SECRET POWER
AND
THE OVERCOMING LIFE

(Two Books)

****

Book 1:
SECRET POWER
OR THE
SECRET OF SUCCESS IN CHRISTIAN LIFE AND WORK"
****

Book 2:
THE OVERCOMING LIFE
AND OTHER SERMONS

****

D. L. MOODY

Trumpet Press Edition, 2023

Copyright 2023 by Trumpet Press

Author: Moody, D. L.

Title: THE SECRET POWER and THE OVERCOMING LIFE

1. Doctrine 2. Bible Studies 3. Theology 4. Faith

ISBN: 978-1-0882-1082-6

Trumpet Press is a Member of the *Christian Indie Publishing Association* (CIPA).

Book 1:

SECRET POWER
OR THE
SECRET OF SUCCESS IN CHRISTIAN LIFE AND WORK"

****

Book 2:

THE OVERCOMING LIFE
AND OTHER SERMONS

Table of Contents

Book 1:

SECRET POWER

PREFACE 5

Chapter 1: POWER — ITS SOURCE 6

Chapter 2: POWER "IN" AND "UPON" 22

Chapter 3: WITNESSING IN POWER. 38

Chapter 4: POWER IN OPERATION 53

Chapter 5: POWER HINDERED..70

Book 2:

THE OVERCOMING LIFE

Chapter 1: THE CHRISTIAN'S WARFARE 81

Chapter 2: INTERNAL FOES 89

Chapter 3: EXTERNAL FOES 98

Chapter 4: RESULTS OF TRUE REPENTANCE 108

Chapter 5: TRUE WISDOM..118

Chapter 6: "COME THOU AND ALL THY HOUSE
                              INTO THE ARK" 128

Chapter 7: HUMILITY 141

Chapter 8: REST 150

Chapter 9: SEVEN "I WILLS" OF CHRIST.......................161

SECRET POWER

OR THE
SECRET OF SUCCESS IN CHRISTIAN LIFE AND WORK"

PREFACE

One man may have "zeal without knowledge," while another may have knowledge without zeal. If I could have only the one, I believe I should choose the first; but, with an open Bible, no one need be without knowledge of God's will and purpose; and the object of this book is to help others to know the source of true power, that both their zeal and their knowledge may be of increased service in the Master's work.

Paul says, "all Scripture is given by inspiration of God, and is profitable;" but I believe one portion, and that the subject of this book, has been too much overlooked, as though it were not practical, and the result is lack of power in testimony and work. If we would work, "not as one that beateth the air," but to some definite purpose, we must have this power from on high. Without this power, our work will be drudgery. With it, it becomes a joyful task, a refreshing service.

May God make this book a blessing to many. This is my prayer.

D. L. MOODY
Northfield, Mass., May 1st, 1881.

CHAPTER 1

POWER — ITS SOURCE

In vain do the inhabitants of London go to their conduits for supply unless the man who has the master-key turns the water on; and in vain do we think to quench our thirst at ordinances, unless God communicates the living water of His Spirit. — *Anon.*

It was the custom of the Roman emperors, at their triumphal entrance, to cast new coins among the multitudes; so doth Christ, in His triumphal ascension into heaven, throw the greatest gifts for the good of men that were ever given. — *T. Goodwin.*

To unconverted persons, a great part of the Bible resembles a letter written in cipher. The blessed Spirit's office is to act as God's decipherer, by letting His people into the secret of celestial experience, as the key and clew to those sweet mysteries of grace which were before as a garden shut up, or as a fountain sealed, or as a book written in an unknown character. — *Toplady.*

The greatest, strongest, mightiest plea for the Church of God in the world is the existence of the Spirit of God in its midst, and the works of the Spirit of God are the true evidences of Christianity. They say miracles are withdrawn, but the Holy Spirit is the standing miracle of the Church of God today. I will not say a word against societies for Christian evidences, nor against those weighty and learned brethren who have defended the outworks of the Christian Church. They have done good service, and I wish them every blessing, but as to my own soul, I never was settled in my faith in Christ by Paley's Evidences, nor by all the evidence ever brought from history or elsewhere; the Holy Spirit has taken the burden off my shoulders, and given me peace and liberty. This to me is evidence, and as to the externals which we can quote to others, it was enough for Peter and John that the people saw the lame man healed, and they needed not to speak for themselves. — *Spurgeon.*

"Without the soul, divinely quickened and inspired, the observances of the grandest ritualism are as worthless as the motions of a galvanized corpse." — *Anon.*

I quote this sentence, as it leads me at once to the subject under consideration. What is this quickening and inspiration? What is this power needed? From whence its source? I reply: The Holy Spirit of God. I am a full believer in "The Apostles' Creed," and therefore "I believe in the Holy Ghost."

A writer has pointedly asked: "What are our souls without His grace? — as dead as the branch in which the sap does not circulate. What is the Church without Him? — as parched and barren as the fields without the dew and rain of heaven."

There has been much inquiry of late on the subject of the Holy Spirit. In this and other lands thousands of persons have been giving attention to the study of this grand theme. I hope it will lead us all to pray for a greater manifestation of His power upon the whole Church of God. How much we have dishonored Him in the past! How ignorant of His grace, and love and presence we have been? True, we have heard of Him and read of Him, but we have had little intelligent knowledge of His attributes, His offices and His relations to us. I fear He has not been to many professed Christians an actual existence, nor is He known to them as a personality of the Godhead.

The first work of the Spirit is to give life; spiritual life. He gives it and He sustains it. If there is no life, there can be no power; Solomon says: "A living dog is better than a dead lion." When the Spirit imparts this life, He does not leave us to droop and die, but constantly fans the flame. He is ever with us. Surely we ought not to be ignorant of His power and his work.

IDENTITY AND PERSONALITY

In John v, 7, we read: "There are three that bear record in heaven, the Father, the Word, and the Holy Ghost, and these three are one." By the Father is meant the first Person, Christ, the Word is the second, and the Holy Spirit, perfectly fulfilling His own office and work in union with the Father and the Son, is the third. I find clearly presented in my Bible, that the One God who demands my love, service and worship, has there revealed Himself, and that each of those three names of Father, Son and Holy Ghost has personality attached to them. Therefore we find some things ascribed to God as Father, some to God as Saviour, and some to God as Comforter and Teacher. It has been remarked that the Father plans, the Son executes, and the Holy Spirit applies. But I also believe they plan and work together. The distinction of persons is often noted in Scripture. In Matt. 3:16-17, we find Jesus submitting to baptism, the Spirit descending upon Him, while the Father's voice of approval is heard saying: "This is my Beloved Son in whom I am well pleased." Again in John 14:16, we read: "I (i.e. Jesus) will pray the Father, and He shall give you another Comforter." Also in Eph. 1:18: "Through Him (i.e. Christ Jesus) we both (Jews and Gentiles) have access by one Spirit unto the Father." Thus we are taught the distinction of persons in the Godhead, and their inseparable union. From these and other scriptures also we learn the identity and actual existence of the Holy Spirit.

If you ask do I understand what is thus revealed in Scripture, I say "no." But my faith bows down before the inspired Word and I unhesitatingly believe the great things of God when even reason is blinded and the intellect confused.

In addition to the teaching of God's Word, the Holy Spirit in His gracious work in the soul declares His own presence. Through His agency we are "born again," and through His indwelling we possess superhuman power. Science, falsely so called, when arrayed against the existence and presence of the Spirit of God with His people, only exposes its own folly to the contempt of those who have become "new creatures in Christ Jesus." The Holy Spirit who inspired prophets, and qualified apostles, continues to animate, guide and comfort all true believers. To the actual Christian, the personality of the Holy Spirit is more real than any theory science has to offer, for so-called science is but calculation based on human observation, and is constantly changing its inferences. But the existence of the Holy Spirit is to the child of God a matter of Scripture revelation and of actual experience.

Some skeptics assert that there is no other vital energy in the world but physical force, while contrary to their assertions, thousands and tens of thousands who can not possibly be deceived have been quickened into spiritual life by a power neither physical or mental. Men who were dead in sins — drunkards who lost their will, blasphemers who lost their purity, libertines sunk in beastliness, infidels who published their shame to the world, have in numberless instances become the subjects of the Spirit's power, and are now walking in the true nobility of Christian manhood, separated by an infinite distance from their former life. Let others reject, if they will, at their own peril, this imperishable truth. I believe, and am growing more into this belief, that divine, miraculous creative power resides in the Holy Ghost. Above and beyond all natural law, yet in harmony with it, creation, providence, the Divine government, and the up-building of the Church of God are presided over by the Spirit of God. His ministration is the ministration of life more glorious than the ministration of law, (2 Cor. 3:6-10). And like the Eternal Son, the Eternal Spirit having life in Himself, is working out all things after the counsel of His own will, and for the everlasting glory of the Triune Godhead.

The Holy Spirit has all the qualities belonging to a person; the power to understand, to will, to do, to call, to feel, to love. This can not be said of a mere influence. He possesses attributes and qualities which can only be ascribed to a person, as acts and deeds are performed by Him which can not be performed by a machine, an influence, or a result.

AGENT AND INSTRUMENT

The Holy Spirit is closely identified with the words of the Lord Jesus. "It is the Spirit that quickeneth; the flesh profiteth nothing, the words that I speak unto you, they are spirit and they are life." The Gospel proclamation can not be divorced from the Holy Spirit. Unless He attend the word in power, vain will be the attempt in preaching it. Human eloquence or persuasiveness of speech are the mere trappings of the dead, if the living Spirit be absent; the prophet may preach to the bones in the valley, but it must be the breath from Heaven which will cause the slain to live.

In the third chapter of the First Epistle of Peter, it reads, "For Christ also hath once suffered for sins, the just for the unjust, that

He might bring us to God, being put to death in the flesh, but quickened by the Spirit."

Here we see that Christ was raised up from the grave by this same Spirit, and the power exercised to raise Christ's dead body must raise our dead souls and quicken them. No other power on earth can quicken a dead soul, but the same power that raised the body of Jesus Christ out of Joseph's sepulcher. And if we want that power to quicken our friends who are dead in sin, we must look to God, and not be looking to man to do it. If we look alone to ministers, if we look alone to Christ's disciples to do this work, we shall be disappointed; but if we look to the Spirit of God and expect it to come from Him and Him alone, then we shall honor the Spirit, and the Spirit will do His work.

SECRET OF EFFICIENCY

I can not help but believe there are many Christians who want to be more efficient in the Lord's service, and the object of this book is to take up this subject of the Holy Spirit, that they may see from whom to expect this power. In the teaching of Christ, we find the last words recorded in the Gospel of Matthew, the 28th chapter and 19th verse, "Go ye, therefore, and teach all nations, baptizing them in the name of the Father, and of the Son, and of the Holy Ghost." Here we find that the Holy Spirit and the Son are equal with the Father — are one with Him, "teaching them in the name of the Father, and of the Son, and of the Holy Ghost." Christ was now handing His commission over to His Apostles. He was going to leave them. His work on earth was finished, and He was now just about ready to take His seat at the right hand of God, and He spoke unto them and said: "All power is given unto Me in heaven and on earth." All power, so then He had authority. If Christ was mere man, as some people try to make out, it would have been blasphemy for Him to have said to the disciples, go and baptize all nations in the name of the Father, and in His own name, and in that of the Holy Ghost, making Himself equal with the Father.

There are three things: All power is given unto Me; go teach all nations. Teach them what? To observe all things. There are a great many people now that are willing to observe what they like about Christ, but the things that they don't like they just dismiss and turn away from. But His commission to His disciples was, "Go teach all nations to observe all things whatsoever I have commanded you." And what right has a messenger who has been sent of God to change the message? If I had sent a servant to deliver a message, and the servant thought the message didn't sound exactly right — a little harsh — and that servant went and changed the message, I should change servants very quickly; he could not serve me any longer. And when a minister or a messenger of Christ begins to change the message because he thinks it is not exactly what it ought to be, and thinks he is wiser than God, God just dismisses that man.

They haven't taught "all things." They have left out some of the things that Christ has commanded us to teach, because they didn't correspond with man's reason. Now we have to take the Word of God just as it is; and if we are going to take it, we have no authority to take out just what we like, what we think is appropriate, and let dark reason be our guide.

It is the work of the Spirit to impress the heart and seal the preached word. His office is to take of the things of Christ and reveal them unto us.

Some people have got an idea that this is the only dispensation of the Holy Ghost; that He didn't work until Christ was glorified. But Simeon felt the Holy Ghost when he went into the temple. In 2 Peter, 1:21, we read: "Holy men of old spake as they were moved by the Holy Ghost." We find the same Spirit in Genesis as is seen in Revelation. The same Spirit that guided the hand that wrote Exodus inspired also the epistles, and we find the same Spirit speaking from one end of the Bible to the other. So holy men in all ages have spoken as they were moved by the Holy Ghost.

HIS PERSONALITY

I was a Christian a long time before I found out that the Holy Ghost was a person. Now this is something a great many don't seem to understand, but if you will just take up the Bible and see what Christ had to say about the Holy Spirit, you will find that He always spoke of Him as a person — never spoke of Him as an influence. Some people have an idea that the Holy Spirit is an attribute of God, just like mercy — just an influence coming from God. But we find in the fourteenth chapter of John, sixteenth verse, these words: "And I will pray the Father, and He shall give you another Comforter that He may abide with you forever." That He may abide with you forever. And, again, in the same chapter, seventeenth verse: "Even the Spirit of Truth, whom the world can not receive, because it seeth Him not, neither knoweth Him; but ye know Him; for He dwelleth with you and shall be in you." Again, in the twenty-sixth verse of the same chapter: "But the Comforter, which is the Holy Ghost, whom the Father will send in my name, He shall teach you all things, and bring all things to your remembrance whatsoever I have said unto you."

Observe the pronouns "He" and "Him." I want to call attention to this fact that whenever Christ spoke of the Holy Ghost He spoke of Him as a person, not a mere influence; and if we want to honor the Holy Ghost, let us bear in mind that He is one of the Trinity, a personality of the Godhead.

THE RESERVOIR OF LOVE

We read that the fruit of the Spirit is love. God is love, Christ is love, and we should not be surprised to read about the love of the Spirit. What a blessed attribute is this. May I call it the dome of the temple of the graces. Better still, it is the crown of crowns worn by the Triune God. Human love is a natural emotion which flows forth towards the object of our affections. But Divine love is as high above human love as the heaven is above the earth. The natural man is of the earth, earthy, and however pure his love may be, it is weak and imperfect at best. But the love of God is perfect and entire, wanting nothing. It is as a mighty ocean in its greatness, dwelling with and flowing from the Eternal Spirit.

In Romans 5:5, we read: "And hope maketh not ashamed, because the love of God is shed abroad in our hearts by the Holy Ghost which is given to us." Now if we are co-workers with God, there is one thing we must possess, and that is love. A man may be a very successful lawyer and have no love for his clients, and yet get on very well. A man may be a very successful physician and have no love for his patients, and yet be a very good physician; a man may be a very successful merchant and have no love for his customers, and yet he may do a good business and succeed; but no man can be a co-worker with God without love. If our service is mere profession on our part, the quicker we renounce it the better. If a man takes up God's work as he would take up any profession, the sooner he gets out of it the better.

We can not work for God without love. It is the only tree that can produce fruit on this sin-cursed earth, that is acceptable to God. If I have no love for God nor for my fellow man, then I can not work acceptably. I am like sounding brass and a tinkling cymbal. We are told that "the love of God is shed abroad in our hearts by the Holy Ghost." Now, if we have had that love shed abroad in our hearts, we are ready for God's service; if we have not, we are not ready. It is so easy to reach a man when you love him; all barriers are broken down and swept away.

Paul when writing to Titus, second chapter and first verse, tells him to be sound in faith, in charity, and in patience. Now in this age, ever since I can remember, the Church has been very jealous about men being unsound in the faith. If a man becomes unsound in the faith, they draw their ecclesiastical sword and cut at him; but he may be ever so unsound in love, and they don't say anything. He may be ever so defective in patience; he may be irritable and fretful all the time, but they never deal with him.

Now the Bible teaches us, that we are not only to be sound in the faith, but in charity and in patience. I believe God can not use many of his servants, because they are full of irritability and impatience; they are fretting all the time, from morning until night. God can not use them; their mouths are sealed; they can not speak for Jesus Christ, and if they have not love, they can not work for God. I do not mean love for those that love me; it don't take grace to do that; the rudest Hottentot in the world can do that; the greatest heathen that ever lived can do that; the vilest man that ever walked the earth can do that. It don't take any grace at all. I did that before I ever became a Christian. Love begets love; hatred begets hatred. If I know a man loves me first, I know my love will be going out towards him. Suppose a man comes to me, saying, "Mr. Moody, a certain man told me today that he thought you were the meanest man living." Well, if I didn't have a good deal of the grace of God in my heart, then I know there would be hard feelings that would spring up in my heart against that man, and it would not be long before I would be talking against him. Hatred begets hatred.

But suppose a man comes to me and says, "Mr. Moody, do you know that such a man that I met today says that he thinks a great deal of you?" and though I may never have heard of him, there would be love springing up in my heart. Love begets love; we all know that; but it takes the grace of God to love the man that lies about me, the man that slanders me, the man that is trying to tear down my character; it takes the grace of God to love that man. You may hate the sin he has committed; there is a difference between the sin and the sinner; you may hate the one with a perfect hatred, but you must love the sinner. I can not otherwise do him any good. Now you know the first impulse of a young convert is to love. Do you remember the day you were converted? Was not your heart full of sweet peace and love?

THE RIGHT OVERFLOW

I remember the morning I came out of my room after I had first trusted Christ, and I thought the old sun shone a good deal brighter than it ever had before; I thought that the sun was just smiling upon me, and I walked out upon Boston Common, and I heard the birds in the trees, and I thought that they were all singing a song for me. Do you know I fell in love with the birds? I never cared for them before; it seemed to me that I was in love with all creation. I had not a bitter feeling against any man, and I was ready to take all men to my heart. If a man has not the love of God shed abroad in his heart, he has never been regenerated. If you hear a person get up in prayer-meeting, and he begins to speak and find fault with everybody, you may know that his is not a genuine conversion; that it is counterfeit; it has not the right ring, because the impulse of a converted soul is to love, and not to be getting up and complaining of every one else, and finding fault. But it is hard for us to live in the right atmosphere all the time. Some one comes along and treats us wrongly, perhaps we hate him; we have not attended to the means of grace and kept feeding on the word of God as we ought; a root of bitterness springs up in our hearts, and perhaps we are not aware of it, but it has come up in our hearts; then we are not qualified to work for God. The love of God is not shed abroad in our hearts as it ought to be by the Holy Ghost.

But the work of the Holy Ghost is to impart love. Paul could say, "The love of Christ constraineth me." He could not help going from town to town and preaching the Gospel. Jeremiah at one time said: "I will speak no more in the Lord's name; I have suffered enough; these people don't like God's word." They lived in a wicked day, as we do now. Infidels were creeping up all around him, who said the word of God was not true; Jeremiah had stood like a wall of fire, confronting them, and he boldly proclaimed that the word of God was true. At last they put him in prison, and he said: "I will keep still; it has cost me too much." But a little while after, you know, he could not keep still. His bones caught fire; he had to speak. And when we are so full of the love of God, we are compelled to work for God, then God blesses us. If our work is sought to be accomplished by the lash, without any true motive power, it will come to nought.

Now the question comes up, have we the love of God shed abroad in our hearts, and are we holding the truth in love? Some people hold the truth, but in such a cold stern way that it will do no good. Other people want to love everything, and so they give up much of the truth; but we are to hold the truth in love; we are to hold the truth even if we lose all, but we are to hold it in love, and if we do that, the Lord will bless us.

There are a good many people trying to get this love; they are trying to produce it of themselves. But therein all fail. The love implanted deep in our new nature will be spontaneous. I don't have to learn to love my children. I can not help loving them. I said to a young miss some time ago, in an inquiry meeting, who said that she could not love God; that it was very hard for her to love Him — I said to her, "Is it hard for you to love your mother? Do you have to learn to love your mother?" And she looked up through her tears, and said, "No; I can't help it; that is spontaneous." "Well," I said, "when the Holy Spirit kindles love in your heart, you can not help loving God; it will be spontaneous." When the Spirit of God comes into your heart and mine, it will be easy to serve God.

The fruit of the Spirit, as you find it in Galatians, begins with love. There are nine graces spoken of in the sixth chapter, and of the nine different graces Paul puts love at the head of the list; love is the first thing — the first in that precious cluster of fruit. Some one has put it in this way: that all the other eight can be put in the word love. Joy is love exulting; peace is love in repose; long suffering is love on trial; gentleness is love in society; goodness is love in action; faith is love on the battlefield; meekness is love at school; and temperance is love in training. So it is love all the way; love at the top; love at the bottom, and all the way along down these graces; and if we only just brought forth the fruit of the Spirit, what a world we would have; there would be no need of any policemen; a man could leave his overcoat around without some one stealing it; men would not have any desire to do evil. Says Paul, "Against such there is no law;" you don't need any law. A man who is full of the Spirit don't need to be put under law; don't need any policemen to watch him. We could dismiss all our policemen; the lawyers would have to give up practicing law, and the courts would not have any business.

THE TRIUMPHS OF HOPE

In the fifteenth chapter of Romans, thirteenth verse, the Apostle says: "Now the God of hope fill you with all joy and peace in believing, that you may abound in hope through the power of the Holy Ghost." The next thing then is hope.

Did you ever notice this, that no man or woman is ever used by God to build up His kingdom who has lost hope? Now, I have been observing this throughout different parts of the country, and wherever I have found a worker in God's vineyard who has lost hope, I have found a man or woman not very useful. Now, just look at these workers. Let your mind go over the past for a moment. Can you think of a man or woman whom God has used to build His kingdom who has lost hope? I don't know of any; I never heard of such an one. It is very important to have hope in the Church; and it is the work of the Holy Ghost to impart hope. Let Him come into some of the churches where there have not been any conversions for a few years, and let Him convert a score of people, and see how hopeful the Church becomes at once. He imparts hope; a man filled with the Spirit of God will be very hopeful. He will be looking out into the future, and he knows that it is all bright, because the God of all grace is able to do great things. So it is very important that we have hope.

If a man has lost hope, he is out of communion with God; he has not the Spirit of God resting upon him for service; he may be a son of God, and disheartened so that he can not be used of God. Do you know there is no place in the Scriptures where it is recorded that God ever used even a discouraged man. Some years ago, in my work I was quite discouraged, and I was ready to hang my harp on the willow. I was very much cast down and depressed. I had been for weeks in that state, when one Monday morning a friend, who had a very large Bible class, came into my study. I used to examine the notes of his Sunday-school lessons, which were equal to a sermon, and he came to me this morning and said, "Well, what did you preach about yesterday?" and I told him. I said, "What did you preach about?" and he said that he preached about Noah. "Did you ever preach about Noah?" "No, I never preached about Noah." "Did you ever study his character?" "No, I never studied his life particularly." "Well," says he, "he is a most wonderful character. It will do you good. You ought to study up that character." When he went out, I took down my Bible, and read about Noah; and then it came over me that Noah worked 120 years and never had a convert, and yet he did not get discouraged; and I said, "Well, I ought not to be discouraged," and I closed my Bible, got up and walked down town, and the cloud had gone.

I went down to the noon prayer-meeting, and heard of a little town in the country where they had taken into the church 100 young converts; and I said to myself, I wonder what Noah would have given if he could have heard that; and yet he worked 120 years and didn't get discouraged. And then a man right across the aisle got up and said, "My friends, I wish you to pray for me; I think I'm lost;" and I thought to myself, "I wonder what Noah would have given to hear that." He never heard a man say, "I wish you to pray for me; I think I am lost," and yet he didn't get discouraged! Oh, children of God, let us not get discouraged; let us ask God to forgive us, if we have been discouraged and cast down; let us ask God to give us hope, that we may be ever hopeful. It does me good sometimes to meet some people and take hold of their hands; they are so hopeful, while other people throw a gloom over me because they are all the time cast down, and looking at the dark side, and looking at the obstacles and difficulties that are in the way.

THE BOON OF LIBERTY

The next thing the Spirit of God does is to give us liberty. He first imparts love; He next inspires hope, and then gives liberty, and that is about the last thing we have in a good many of our churches at the present day. And I am sorry to say there must be a funeral in a good many churches before there is much work done, we shall have to bury the formalism so deep that it will never have any resurrection. The last thing to be found in many a church is liberty.

If the Gospel happens to be preached, the people criticize, as they would a theatrical performance. It is exactly the same, and many a professed Christian never thinks of listening to what the man of God has to say. It is hard work to preach to carnally-minded critics, but "Where the spirit of the Lord is, there is liberty."

Very often a woman will hear a hundred good things in a sermon, and there may be one thing that strikes her as a little out of place, and she will go home and sit down to the table and talk right out before her children and magnify that one wrong thing, and not say a word about the hundred good things that were said. That is what people do who criticize.

God does not use men in captivity. The condition of many is like Lazarus when he came out of the sepulcher bound hand and foot. The bandage was not taken off his mouth, and he could not speak. He had life, and if you had said Lazarus was not alive, you would have told a falsehood, because he was raised from the dead. There are a great many people, the moment you talk to them and insinuate they are not doing what they might, they say: "I have life. I am a Christian." Well, you can't deny it, but they are bound hand and foot.

May God snap these fetters and set His children free, that they may have liberty. I believe He comes to set us free, and wants us to work for Him, and speak for Him. How many people would like to get up in a social prayer-meeting to say a few words for Christ, but there is such a cold spirit of criticism in the Church that they dare not do it. They have not the liberty to do it. If they get up, they are so frightened with these critics that they begin to tremble and sit down. They can not say anything. Now, that is all wrong. The Spirit of God comes just to give liberty, and wherever you see the Lord's work going on, you will see that Spirit of liberty. People won't be afraid of speaking to one another. And when the meeting is over they will not get their hats and see how quick they can get out of the church, but will begin to shake hands with one another, and there will be liberty there. A good many go to the prayer-meeting out of a mere cold sense of duty. They think "I must attend because I feel it is my duty." They don't think it is a glorious privilege to meet and pray, and to be strengthened, and to help some one else in the wilderness journey.

What we need today is love in our hearts. Don't we want it? Don't we want hope in our lives? Don't we want to be hopeful? Don't we want liberty? Now, all this is the work of the Spirit of God, and let us pray God daily to give us love, and hope, and liberty. We read in Hebrews, "Having, therefore, brethren, boldness to enter into the holiest by the blood of Jesus." If you will turn to the passage and read the margin — it says: "Having, therefore, brethren, liberty to enter into the holiest." We can go into the holiest, having freedom of access, and plead for this love and liberty and glorious hope, that we may not rest until God gives us the power to work for Him.

If I know my own heart today, I would rather die than live as I once did, a mere nominal Christian, and not used by God in building up His kingdom. It seems a poor empty life to live for the sake of self.

Let us seek to be useful. Let us seek to be vessels meet for the Master's use, that God, the Holy Spirit, may shine fully through us.

"Know, my soul, thy full salvation;
Rise o'er sin, and fear, and care;
Joy to find, in every station,
Something still to do or bear.

Think what Spirit dwells within thee;

Think what Father's smiles are thine;
Think that Jesus died to win thee:
Child of heaven, canst thou repine?

Haste thee on from grace to glory,
Armed by faith, and winged by prayer,
Heaven's eternal day's before thee:
God's own hand shall guide thee there.

Soon shall close thy earthly mission,
Soon shall pass thy pilgrim days,
Hope shall change to glad fruition,
Faith to sight, and prayer to praise."

"I am so weak, dear Lord! I can not stand
One moment without Thee;
But oh, the tenderness of Thy enfolding,
And oh, the faithfulness of Thine upholding,
And oh, the strength of Thy right hand!
That strength is enough for me.

I am so needy, Lord! and yet I know
All fullness dwells in Thee;
And hour by hour that never-failing treasure
Supplies and fills in overflowing measure
My last and greatest need. And so
Thy grace is enough for me.

It is so sweet to trust Thy word alone!
I do not ask to see
The unveiling of Thy purpose, or the shining
Of future light on mysteries untwining;
Thy promise-roll is all my own —
Thy word is enough for me.

There were strange soul-depths, restless, vast, and broad,

Unfathomed as the sea,
An infinite craving for some infinite stilling;
But now Thy perfect love is perfect filling!
Lord Jesus Christ, my Lord, my God,
Thou, Thou art enough for me!"

CHAPTER 2

POWER "IN" AND "UPON"

> You remember that strange, half-involuntary "forty years" of Moses in the "wilderness" of Midian, when he had fled from Egypt. You remember, too, the almost equally strange years of retirement in "Arabia" by Paul, when, if ever, humanly speaking, instant action was needed. And pre-eminently you remember the amazing charge of the ascending Lord to the disciples, "Tarry at Jerusalem." Speaking after the manner of men, one could not have wondered if out-spoken Peter, or fervid James had said: "Tarry, Lord! How long?" "Tarry, Lord! is there not a perishing world, groaning for the 'good news?'" "Tarry! did we hear Thee aright, Lord? Was the word not haste?" "Nay;" "Being assembled together with them, He commanded them that they should not depart from Jerusalem, but wait for the promise of the Father." (Acts 1:4.) — *Grosart.*

The Holy Spirit dwelling in us, is one thing; I think this is clearly brought out in Scripture; and the Holy Spirit upon us for service, is another thing. Now there are only three places we find in Scripture that are dwelling-places for the Holy Ghost.

In the 40th chapter of Exodus, commencing with the 33d verse, are these words:

> "And he (that is Moses) reared up the court round about the tabernacle and the altar, and set up the hanging of the court gate. So Moses finished the work.
>
> Then a cloud covered the tent of the congregation, and the glory of the Lord filled the tabernacle.
>
> And Moses was not able to enter into the tent of the congregation, because the cloud abode thereon, and the glory of the Lord filled the tabernacle."

The moment that Moses finished the work, the moment that the tabernacle was ready, the cloud came, the Shekinah glory came and filled it so that Moses was not able to stand before the presence of the Lord. I believe firmly, that the moment our hearts are emptied of pride and selfishness and ambition and self-seeking, and everything that is contrary to God's law, the Holy Ghost will come and fill every corner of our hearts; but if we are full of pride and conceit, and ambition and self-seeking, and pleasure and the world, there is no room for the Spirit of God; and I believe many a man is praying to God to fill him when he is full already with something else. Before we pray that God would fill us, I believe we ought to pray Him to empty us.

There must be an emptying before there can be a filling; and when the heart is turned upside down, and everything is turned out that is contrary to God, then the Spirit will come, just as He did in the tabernacle, and fill us with His glory. We read in 2d Chronicles, 5th chapter and 13th verse:

> "It came even to pass, as the trumpeters and singers were as one to make one Sound, to be heard in praising and thanking the Lord, and when they lifted up their voice with the trumpets and cymbals and instruments of music, and praised the Lord, saying, For He is good; for His mercy endureth forever; that then the house was filled with a cloud, even the house of the Lord. So that the priests could not stand to minister by reason of the cloud, for the glory of the Lord had filled the house of God."

PRAISING WITH ONE HEART

We find, the very moment that Solomon completed the Temple, when all was finished, they were just praising God with one heart — the choristers and the singers and the ministers were all one; there was not any discord; they were all praising God, and the glory of God came and just filled the Temple as the Tabernacle. Now, as you turn over into the New Testament, you will find, instead of coming to Tabernacles and Temples, believers are now the Temple of the Holy Ghost. When, on the day of Pentecost, before Peter preached that memorable sermon, as they were praying, the Holy Ghost came, and came in mighty power. We now pray for the Spirit of God to come, and we sing:

"Come, Holy Spirit, heavenly dove,
With all thy quickening power;
Kindle a flame of heavenly love
In these cold hearts of ours,"

I believe, if we understand it, it is perfectly right; but if we are praying for Him to come out of heaven down to earth again, that is wrong, because He is already here; He has not been out of this earth for 1800 years; He has been in the Church, and He is with all believers; the believers in the Church are the called-out ones; they are called out from the world, and every true believer is a Temple for the Holy Ghost to dwell in. In the 14th chapter of John, 17th verse, we have the words of Jesus:

> "The Spirit of Truth, whom the world can not receive, because it seeth Him not, neither knoweth Him; but ye know Him, for He dwelleth in you."

"Greater is He that is in you than He that is in the world." If we have the Spirit dwelling in us, He gives us power over the flesh and the world, and over every enemy. "He is dwelling with you, and shall be in you."

Read 1st Corinthians 3:16: "Know ye not that ye are the temple of God, and that the Spirit of God dwelleth in you?"

There were some men burying an aged saint some time ago, and he was very poor, like many of God's people, poor in this world, but they are very rich, they have all the riches on the other side of life — they have them laid up there where thieves can not get them, and where sharpers can not take them away from them, and where moth can not corrupt — so this aged man was very rich in the other world, and they were just hastening him off to the grave, wanting to get rid of him, when an old minister, who was officiating at the grave, said, "Tread softly, for you are carrying the temple of the Holy Ghost." Whenever you see a believer, you see a temple of the Holy Ghost.

In 1 Cor. 6:19, 20, we read again: "Know ye not that your body is the temple of the Holy Ghost which is in you, which ye have of God, and ye are not your own for ye are bought with a price, therefore glorify God in your body and in your spirit, which are God's." Thus are we taught that there is a divine resident in every child of God.

I think it is clearly taught in the Scripture that every believer has the Holy Ghost dwelling in him. He may be quenching the Spirit of God, and he may not glorify God as he should, but if he is a believer on the Lord Jesus Christ, the Holy Ghost dwells in him. But I want to call your attention to another fact. I believe today, that though Christian men and women have the Holy Spirit dwelling in them, yet He is not dwelling within them in power; in other words, God has a great many sons and daughters without power.

WHAT IS NEEDED

Nine-tenths, at least, of the church members never think of speaking for Christ. If they see a man, perhaps a near relative, just going right down to ruin, going rapidly, they never think of speaking to him about his sinful course and of seeking to win him to Christ. Now certainly there must be something wrong. And yet when you talk with them you find they have faith, and you can not say they are not children of God; but they have not the power, they have not the liberty, they have not the love that real disciples of Christ should have.

A great many people are thinking that we need new measures, that we need new churches, that we need new organs, and that we need new choirs, and all these new things. That is not what the Church of God needs today. It is the old power that the Apostles had; that is what we want, and if we have that in our churches, there will be new life. Then we will have new ministers — the same old ministers renewed with power; filled with the Spirit. I remember when in Chicago many were toiling in the work, and it seemed as though the car of salvation didn't move on, when a minister began to cry out from the very depths of his heart, "Oh, God, put new ministers in every pulpit." On next Monday I heard two or three men stand up and say, "We had a new minister last Sunday — the same old minister, but he had got new power," and I firmly believe that is what we want today all over America. We want new ministers in the pulpit and new people in the pews. We want people quickened by the Spirit of God, and the Spirit coming down and taking possession of the children of God and giving them power.

Then a man filled with the Spirit will know how to use "the sword of the Spirit." If a man is not filled with the Spirit, he will never know now to use the Book. We are told that this is the sword of the Spirit; and what is an army good for that does not know how to use its weapons? Suppose a battle going on, and I were a general and had a hundred thousand men, great, able-bodied men, full of life, but they could not one of them handle a sword, and not one of them knew how to use his rifle, what would that army be good for? Why, one thousand well-drilled men, with good weapons, would rout the whole of them. The reason why the Church can not overcome the enemy is, because she don't know how to use the sword of the Spirit. People will get up and try to fight the devil with their experiences, but he don't care for that, he will overcome them every time. People are trying to fight the devil with theories and pet ideas, but he will get the victory over them likewise. What we want is to draw the sword of the Spirit. It is that which cuts deeper than anything else.

Turn in your Bibles to Eph. 6:14: "Stand, therefore, having your loins girt about with truth, and having on the breastplate of righteousness; and your feet shod with the preparation of the gospel of peace; above all (or over all), taking the shield of faith, wherewith ye shall be able to quench all the fiery darts of the wicked. And take the helmet of salvation and the sword of the Spirit, which is the Word of God."

THE GREATEST WEAPON

The sword of the Spirit is the Word of God, and what we need specially is to be filled with the Spirit, so we shall know how to use the Word. There was a Christian man talking to a skeptic, who was using the Word, and the skeptic said, "I don't believe, sir, in that Book." But the man went right on and he gave him more of the Word; and the man again remarked, "I don't believe the Word," but he kept giving him more, and at last the man was reached. And the brother added, "When I have proved a good sword which does the work of execution, I would just keep right on using it." That is what we want. Skeptics and infidels may say they don't believe in it. It is not our work to make them believe in it; that is the work of the Spirit. Our work is to give them the Word of God; not to preach our theories and our ideas about it, but just to deliver the message as God gives it to us. We read in the Scriptures of the sword of the Lord and Gideon.

Suppose Gideon had gone out without the Word, he would have been defeated. But the Lord used Gideon; and I think you find all through the Scriptures, God takes up and uses human instruments. You can not find, I believe, a case in the Bible where a man is converted without God calling in some human agency — using some human instrument; not but what He can do it in His independent sovereignty; there is no doubt about that. Even when by the revealed glory of the Lord Jesus, Saul of Tarsus was smitten to the earth, Annanias was used to open his eyes and lead him into the light of the Gospel. I heard a man once say, if you put a man on a mountain peak, higher than one of the Alpine peaks, God could save him without a human messenger; but that is not His way; that is not His method; but it is "the sword of the Lord and Gideon"; and the Lord and Gideon will do the work; and if we are just willing to let the Lord use us, He will.

"NONE OF SELF"

Then you will find all through the Scriptures, when men were filled with the Holy Spirit, they preached Christ and not themselves. They preached Christ and Him crucified. It says in the first chapter of Luke, 67th verse, speaking of Zacharias, the father of John the Baptist:

> "And his father, Zacharias, was filled with the Holy Ghost, and prophesied, saying: Blessed be the Lord God of Israel, for He hath visited and redeemed His people, and hath raised up an horn of salvation for us in the house of His servant David. As He spake by the mouth of His Holy prophets, which have been since the world began."

See, he is talking about the Word. If a man is filled with the Spirit, he will magnify the Word; he will preach the Word, and not himself; he will give this lost world the Word of the living God. "And thou, child, shalt be called the prophet of the Highest; for thou shalt go before the face of the Lord to prepare His ways. To give knowledge of salvation unto His people by the remission of their sins, through the tender mercy of our God, whereby the dayspring from on high hath visited us. To give light to them that sit in darkness and in the shadow of death, to guide our feet into the way of peace. And the child grew and waxed strong in spirit, and was in the deserts till the day of his showing unto Israel." And so we find again that when Elizabeth and Mary met, they talked of the Scriptures, and they were both filled with the Holy Ghost, and at once began to talk of their Lord.

We also find that Simeon, as he came into the temple and found the young child Jesus there, at once began to quote the Scriptures, for the Spirit was upon him. And when Peter stood up on the day of Pentecost, and preached that wonderful sermon, it is said he was filled with the Holy Ghost, and began to preach the Word to the multitude, and it was the Word that cut them. It was the sword of the Lord and Peter, the same as it was the sword of the Lord and Gideon. And we find it says of Stephen, "They were not able to resist the spirit and wisdom by which he spake." Why? Because he gave them the Word of God. And we are told that the Holy Ghost came on Stephen, and none could resist his word. And we read, too, that Paul was full of the Holy Spirit, and that he preached Christ and Him crucified, and that many people were added to the Church. Barnabas was full of faith and the Holy Ghost; and if you will just read and find out what he preached, you will find it was the Word, and many were added to the Lord. So that when a man is full of the Spirit, he begins to preach, not himself, but Christ, as revealed in the Holy Scriptures.

The disciples of Jesus were all filled with the Spirit, and the Word was published; and when the Spirit of God comes down upon the Church, and we are anointed, the Word will be published in the streets, in the lanes, and in the alleys; there will not be a dark cellar nor a dark attic, nor a home where the Gospel will not be carried by some loving heart, if the Spirit comes upon God's people in demonstration and in power.

SPIRITUAL IRRIGATION

It is possible a man may just barely have life and be satisfied; and I think that a great many are in that condition. In the 3d chapter of John we find that Nicodemus came to Christ and that he received life. At first this life was feeble. You don't hear of him standing up confessing Christ boldly, and of the Spirit coming upon him in great power, though possessing life through faith in

Christ. And then turn to the 4th chapter of John, and you will find it speaks of the woman coming to the well of Samaria, and Christ held out the cup of salvation to her and she took it and drank, and it became in her "a well of water springing up into everlasting life." That is better than in the 3d chapter of John; here it came down in a flood into her soul; as some one has said, it came down from the throne of God, and like a mighty current carried her back to the throne of God. Water always rises to its level, and if we get the soul filled with water from the throne of God it will bear us upward to its source.

But if you want to get the best class of Christian life portrayed, turn to the 7th chapter and you will find that it says he that receiveth the Spirit, through trusting in the Lord Jesus, "out of him shall flow rivers of living water." Now there are two ways of digging a well. I remember, when a boy, upon a farm, in New England, they had a well, and they put in an old wooden pump, and I used to have to pump the water from that well upon wash-day, and to water the cattle; and I had to pump and pump and pump until my arm got tired, many a time. But they have a better way now; they don't dig down a few feet and brick up the hole and put the pump in, but they go down through the clay and the sand and the rock, and on down until they strike what they call a lower stream, and then it becomes an artesian well, which needs no labor, as the water rises spontaneously from the depths beneath.

Now I think God wants all His children to be a sort of artesian well; not to keep pumping, but to flow right out. Why, haven't you seen ministers in the pulpit just pumping, and pumping and pumping? I have, many a time, and I have had to do it, too. I know how it is. They stand in the pulpit and talk and talk and talk, and the people go to sleep, they can't arouse them. What is the trouble? Why, the living water is not there; they are just pumping when there is no water in the well. You can't get water out of a dry well; you have to get something in the well, or you can't get anything out. I have seen these wooden pumps where you had to pour water into them before you could pump any water out, and so it is with a good many people; you have to get something in them before you can get any out. People wonder why it is that they have no Spiritual power. They stand up and talk in meeting, and don't say anything; they say they haven't anything to say, and you find it out soon enough; they need not state it; but they just talk, because they feel it is a duty, and say nothing.

Now I tell you when the Spirit of God is on us for service, resting upon us, we are anointed, and then we can do great things. "I will pour water on him that is thirsty," says God. O, blessed thought — "He that hungers and thirsts after righteousness shall be filled!"

OUTFLOWING STREAMS

I would like to see some one just full of living water; so full that they couldn't contain it; that they would have to go out and publish the Gospel of the grace of God. When a man gets so full that he can't hold any more, then he is just ready for God's service.

When preaching in Chicago, Dr. Gibson remarked in the inquiry meeting, "Now, how can we find out who is thirsty?" Said he, "I was just thinking how we could find out. If a boy should come down the aisle, bringing a good pail full of clear water, and a dipper, we would soon find out who was thirsty; we would see thirsty men and women reach out for water; but if you should walk down the aisle with an empty bucket, you wouldn't find it out. People would look in and see that there was no water, and say nothing." So said he, "I think that is the reason we are not more blessed in our ministry; we are carrying around empty buckets, and the people see that we have not anything in them, and they don't come forward."

I think that there is a good deal of truth in that. People see that we are carrying around empty buckets, and they will not come to us until they are filled. They see we haven't any more than they have. We must have the Spirit of God resting upon us, and then we will have something that gives the victory over the world, the flesh, and the devil; something that gives the victory over our tempers, over our conceits, and over every other evil, and when we can trample these sins under our feet, then people will come to us and say, "How did you get it? I need this power; you have something that I haven't got; I want it." O, may God show us this truth. Have we been toiling all night? let us throw the net on the right side; let us ask God to forgive our sins, and anoint us with power from on high. But remember, He is not going to give this power to an impatient man; He is not going to give it to a selfish man; He will never give it to an ambitious man whose aim is selfish, till first emptied of self; emptied of pride and of all worldly thoughts. Let it be God's glory and not our own that we seek, and when we get to that point, how speedily the Lord will bless us for good. Then will the measure of our blessing be full. Do you know what heaven's measure is? Good measure, pressed down, shaken together, and running over.

If we get our heart filled with the Word of God, how is Satan going to get in? How is the world going to get in, for heaven's measure is good measure, full measure, running over. Have you this fullness? If you have not, then seek it; say by the grace of God you will have it, for it is the Father's good pleasure to give us these things. He wants us to shine down in this world; He wants to lift us up for His work; He wants us to have the power to testify for His Son. He has left us in this world to testify for Him. What did He leave us for? Not to buy and sell and to get gain, but to glorify Christ. How are you going to do it without the Spirit? That is the question. How are you to do it without the power of God?

WHY SOME FAIL

We read in John 20:22: "And when He had said this, He breathed on them, and saith unto them, Receive ye the Holy Ghost."

Then see Luke 24:49: "And, behold, I send the promise of my Father upon you; but tarry ye in the city of Jerusalem until ye be endued with power from on high."

The first passage tells us He had raised those pierced and wounded hands over them and breathed upon them and said, "Receive ye the Holy Ghost." And I haven't a doubt they received it then, but not in such mighty power as afterward when qualified for their work. It was not in fullness that He gave it to them then, but if they had been like a good many now, they would have said, "I have enough now; I am not going to tarry; I am going to work."

Some people seem to think they are losing time if they wait on God for his power, and so away they go and work without unction; they are working without any anointing, they are working without any power. But after Jesus had said "Receive ye the Holy Ghost," and had breathed on them, He said: "Now you tarry in Jerusalem until you be endued with power from on high." Read in the 1st chapter of Acts, 8th verse: "But ye shall receive power, after that the Holy Ghost is come upon you."

Now, the Spirit had been given them certainly or they could not have believed, and they could not have taken their stand for God and gone through what they did, and endured the scoffs and frowns of their friends, if they had not been converted by the power of the Holy Ghost. But now just see what Christ said:

> "Ye shall receive power after that the Holy Ghost is come upon you; and ye shall be witnesses unto me both in Jerusalem and in all Judea, and in Samaria, and unto the uttermost parts of the earth."

Then, the Holy Spirit in us is one thing, and the Holy Spirit on us is another; and if these Christians had gone out and went right to preaching then and there, without the power, do you think that scene would have taken place on the day of Pentecost? Don't you think that Peter would have stood up there and beat against the air, while these Jews would have gnashed their teeth and mocked him? But they tarried in Jerusalem; they waited ten days. What! you say. What, the world perishing and men dying! Shall I wait? Do what God tells you. There is no use in running before you are sent; there is no use in attempting to do God's work without God's power. A man working without this unction, a man working without this anointing, a man working without the Holy Ghost upon him, is losing his time after all. So we are not going to lose anything if we tarry till we get this power. That is the object of true service, to wait on God, to tarry till we receive this power for witness-bearing. Then we find that on the day of Pentecost, ten days after Jesus Christ was glorified, the Holy Spirit descended in power. Do you think that Peter and James and John and those apostles doubted it from that very hour? They never doubted it. Perhaps some question the possibility of having the power of God now, and that the Holy Spirit never came afterward in similar manifestation, and will never come again in such power.

FRESH SUPPLIES

Turn to Acts 4:31, and you will find He came a second time, and at a place where they were, so that the earth was shaken, and they were filled with this power. The fact is, we are leaky vessels, and we have to keep right under the fountain all the time to keep full of Christ, and so have a fresh supply.

I believe this is a mistake a great many of us are making; we are trying to do God's work with the grace God gave us ten years ago. We say, if it is necessary, we will go on with the same grace. Now, what we want is a fresh supply, a fresh anointing and fresh power, and if we seek it, and seek it with all our hearts, we will obtain it. The early converts were taught to look for that power.

Philip went to Samaria, and news reached Jerusalem that there was a great work being done in Samaria, and many converts; and John and Peter went down, and they laid their hands on them, and they received the Holy Ghost for service. I think that is what we Christians ought to be looking for — the Spirit of God for service — that God may use us mightily in the building up of His Church and hastening His glory. In Acts xix we read of twelve men at Ephesus, who, when the inquiry was made if they had received the Holy Ghost since they believed, answered: "We have not so much as heard whether there be any Holy Ghost." I venture to say there are very many, who, if you were to ask them, "Have you received the Holy Ghost since you believed?" would reply, "I don't know what you mean by that." They would be like the twelve men down at Ephesus, who had never understood the peculiar relation of the Spirit to the sons of God in this dispensation. I firmly believe that the Church has just laid this knowledge aside, mislaid it somewhere, and so Christians are without power. Sometimes you can take one hundred members into the Church, and they don't add to its power. Now that is all wrong. If they were only anointed by the Spirit of God, there would be great power if one hundred saved ones were added to the Church.

GREEN FIELDS

When I was out in California, the first time I went down from the Sierra Nevada Mountains and dropped into the Valley of the Sacramento, I was surprised to find on one farm that everything about it was green — all the trees and flowers, everything was blooming, and everything was green and beautiful, and just across the hedge everything was dried up, and there was not a green thing there, and I could not understand it; I made inquiries, and I found that the man that had everything green, irrigated; he just poured the water right on, and he kept everything green, while the fields that were next to his were as dry as Gideon's fleece without a drop of dew; and so it is with a great many in the Church today. They are like these farms in California — a dreary desert, everything parched and desolate, and apparently no life in them. They can sit next to a man who is full of the Spirit of God, who is like a green bay tree, and who is bringing forth fruit, and yet they will not seek a similar blessing. Well, why this difference? Because God has poured water on him that was thirsty; that is the difference. One has been seeking this anointing, and he has received it; and when we want this above everything else God will surely give it to us.

The great question before us now is, Do we want it? I remember when I first went to England and gave a Bible reading, I think about the first that I gave in that country, a great many ministers were there, and I didn't know anything about English theology, and I was afraid I should run against their creeds, and I was a little hampered, especially on this very subject, about the gift of the Holy Spirit for service.

I remember particularly a Christian minister there who had his head bowed on his hand, and I thought the good man was ashamed of everything I was saying, and of course that troubled me. At the close of my address he took his hat and away he went, and then I thought, "Well, I shall never see him again." At the next meeting I looked all around for him and he wasn't there, and at the next meeting I looked again, but he was absent; and I thought my teaching must have given him offense. But a few days after that, at a large noon prayer meeting, a man stood up and his face shone as if he had been up in the mountain with God, and I looked at him, and to my great joy it was this brother. He said he was at that Bible reading, and he heard there was such a thing as having fresh power to preach the Gospel; he said he made up his mind that if that was for him he would have it; he said he went home and looked to the Master, and that he never had such a battle with himself in his life. He asked that God would show him the sinfulness of his heart that he knew nothing about, and he just cried mightily to God that he might be emptied of himself and filled with the Spirit, and he said, "God has answered my prayer."

I met him in Edinburgh six months from that date, and he told me he had preached the Gospel every night during that time, that he had not preached one sermon but that some remained for conversation, and that he had engagements four months ahead to preach the Gospel every night in different churches. I think you could have fired a cannon ball right through his church and not hit any one before he got this anointing; but it was not thirty days before the building was full and aisles crowded. He had his bucket filled full of fresh water, and the people found it out and came flocking to him from every quarter.

I tell you, you can't get the stream higher than the fountain. What we need very specially is power.

There was another man whom I have in my mind, and he said, "I have heart disease, I can't preach more than once a week," so he had a colleague to preach for him and do the visiting. He was an old minister, and he couldn't do any visiting. He had heard of this anointing, and said, "I would like to be anointed for my burial. I would like before I go hence to have just one more privilege to preach the Gospel with power." He prayed that God would fill him with the Spirit, and I met him not long after that, and he said, "I have preached on an average eight times a week, and I have had conversions all along." The Spirit came on him. I don't believe that man broke down at first with hard work, so much as with using the machinery without oil, without lubrication. It is not the hard work breaks down ministers, but it is the toil of working without power. Oh, that God may anoint His people! Not the ministry only, but every disciple. Do not suppose pastors are the only laborers needing it. There is not a mother but needs it in her house to regulate her family, just as much as the minister needs it in the pulpit or the Sunday-school teacher needs it in his Sunday-school. We all need it together, and let us not rest day nor night until we possess it; if that is the uppermost thought in our hearts, God will give it to us if we just hunger and thirst for it, and say, "God helping me, I will not rest until endued with power from on high."

MASTER AND SERVANT

There is a very sweet story of Elijah and Elisha, and I love to dwell upon it. The time had come for Elijah to be taken up, and he said to Elisha, "You stay here at Gilgal, and I will go up to Bethel." There was a theological seminary there, and some young students, and he wanted to see how they were getting along; but Elisha said, "As the Lord liveth, and thy soul liveth, I will not leave thee." And so Elisha just kept close to Elijah. They came to Bethel, and the sons of the prophets came out and said to Elisha, "Do you know that your master is to be taken away?" And Elisha said, "I know it; but you keep still." Then Elijah said to Elisha, "You remain at Bethel until I go to Jericho." But Elisha said, "As the Lord liveth and my soul liveth, I will not leave thee." "You shall not go without me," says Elisha; and then I can imagine that Elisha just put his arm in that of Elijah, and they walked down together. I can see those two mighty men walking down to Jericho, and when they arrived there, the sons of the prophets came and said to Elisha, "Do you know that your master is to be taken away?" "Hush! keep still," says Elisha, "I know it." And then Elijah said to Elisha, "Tarry here awhile; for the Lord hath sent me to Jordan." But Elisha said, "As the Lord liveth and my soul liveth, I will not leave thee. You shall not go without me." And then Elisha came right close to Elijah, and as they went walking down, I imagine Elisha was after something; when they came to the Jordan, Elijah took off his mantle and struck the waters, and they separated hither and thither, and the two passed through like giants, dryshod, and fifty sons of the prophets came to look at them and watch them.

They didn't know but Elijah would be taken up right in their sight. As they passed over Jordan, Elijah said to Elisha, "Now, what do you want?" He knew he was after something. "What can I do for you. Just make your request known." And he said, "I would like a double portion of thy Spirit." I can imagine now that Elijah had given him a chance to ask; he said to himself, "I will ask for enough." Elisha had a good deal of the Spirit, but, says he, "I want a double portion of thy Spirit." "Well," says Elijah, "if you see me when I am taken up, you shall have it." Do you think you could have enticed Elisha from Elijah at that moment? I can almost see the two arm in arm, walking along, and as they walked, there came along the chariot of fire, and before Elisha knew it, Elijah was caught up, and as he went sweeping towards the throne, the servant cried, "My Father! My Father! The chariot of Israel and the horsemen thereof!" Elisha saw him no more. He picked up Elijah's fallen mantle, and returning with that old mantle of his master's, he came to the Jordan and cried for Elijah's God, and the waters separated hither and thither, and he passed through dryshod. Then the watching prophets lifted up their voices and said, "The Spirit of Elijah is upon Elisha;" and so it was, a double portion of it.

May the Spirit of Elijah, beloved reader, be upon us. If we seek for it we will have it. Oh, may the God of Elijah answer by fire, and consume the spirit of worldliness in the churches, burn up the dross, and make us whole-hearted Christians. May that Spirit come upon us; let that be our prayer in our family altars and in our closets. Let us cry mightily to God that we may have a double portion of the Holy Spirit, and that we may not rest satisfied with this worldly state of living, but let us, like Sampson, shake ourselves and come out from the world, that we may have the power of God.

CHAPTER 3

WITNESSING IN POWER.

A man may as well hew marble without tools, or paint without colors or instruments, or build without materials, as perform any acceptable service without the graces of the Spirit, which are both the materials and the instruments in the work. — *Alleine.*

If we do not have the Spirit of God, it were better to shut the churches, to nail up the doors, to put a black cross on them, and say, "God have mercy on us!" If you ministers have not the Spirit of God, you had better not preach, and you people had better stay at home. I think I speak not too strongly when I say that a church in the land without the Spirit of God is rather a curse than a blessing. If you have not the Spirit of God, Christian worker, remember that you stand in somebody else's way; you are as a tree bearing no fruit standing where another fruitful tree might grow. This is solemn work; the Holy Spirit or nothing, and worse than nothing. Death and condemnation to a church that is not yearning after the Spirit, and crying and groaning until the Spirit has wrought mightily in her midst. He is here; He has never gone back since He descended at Pentecost. He is often grieved and vexed, for He is peculiarly jealous and sensitive, and the one sin never forgiven has to do with His blessed person; therefore let us be very tender towards Him, walk humbly before Him, wait on Him very earnestly, and resolve that about us there should be nothing knowingly continued which should prevent Him dwelling in us, and being with us henceforth and for, ever. Brethren, peace be unto you and your spirit! — *Spurgeon.*

WITNESSING IN POWER

The subject of witness-bearing in the power of the Holy Ghost is not sufficiently understood by the Church. Until we have more intelligence on this point we are laboring under great disadvantage. Now, if you will take your Bible and turn to the 15th chapter of John and the 26th verse, you will find these words: "But when the Comforter is come, whom I will send unto you from the Father, even the Spirit of Truth, which proceedeth from the Father, He shall testify of me; and ye also shall bear witness, because ye have been with me from the beginning." Here we find what the Spirit is going to do, or what Christ said He would do when He came; namely, that He should testify of Him. And if you will turn over to the second chapter of Acts you will find that when Peter stood up on the day of Pentecost, and testified of what Christ had done, the Holy Spirit came down and bore witness to that fact, and men were convicted by hundreds and by thousands. So then man can not preach effectively of himself. He must have the Spirit of God to give ability, and study God's Word in order to testify according to the mind of the Spirit.

WHAT IS THE TESTIMONY?

If we keep back the Gospel of Christ and do not bring Christ before the people, then the Spirit has not the opportunity to work. But the moment Peter stood up on the day of Pentecost and bore testimony to this one fact, that Christ died for sin, and that He had been raised again, and ascended into heaven — the Spirit came down to bear witness to the Person and Work of Christ.

He came down to bear witness to the fact that Christ was in heaven, and if it was not for the Holy Ghost bearing witness to the preaching of the facts of the Gospel, do you think that the Church would have lived during these last eighteen centuries? Do you believe that Christ's death, resurrection and ascension would not have been forgotten as soon as His birth, if it had not been for the fact that the Holy Spirit had come? Because it is very clear, that when John made his appearance on the borders of the wilderness, they had forgotten all about the birth of Jesus Christ. Just thirty short years. It was all gone. They had forgotten the story of the Shepherds; they had forgotten the wonderful scene that took place in the temple, when the Son of God was brought into the temple and the older prophets and prophetesses were there; they had forgotten about the wise men coming to Jerusalem to inquire where

He was that was born King of the Jews. That story of His birth seemed to have just faded away; they had forgotten all about it, and when John made his appearance on the borders of the wilderness it was brought back to their minds. And if it had not been for the Holy Ghost coming down to bear witness to Christ, to testify of His death and resurrection, these facts would have been forgotten as soon as His birth.

GREATER WORK

The witness of the Spirit is the witness of power. Jesus said, "The works that I do shall ye do also, and greater works than these shall ye do because I go to the Father." I used to stumble over that. I didn't understand it. I thought, what greater work could any man do than Christ had done? How could any one raise a dead man who had been laid away in the sepulcher for days, and who had already begun to turn back to dust; how with a word could he call him forth? But the longer I live the more I am convinced it is a greater thing to influence a man's will; a man whose will is set against God; to have that will broken and brought into subjection to God's will — or, in other words, it is a greater thing to have power over a living, sinning, God-hating man, than to quicken the dead. He who could create a world could speak a dead soul into life; but I think the greatest miracle this world has ever seen was the miracle at Pentecost. Here were men who surrounded the Apostles, full of prejudice, full of malice, full of bitterness, their hands, as it were, dripping with the blood of the Son of God, and yet an unlettered man, a man whom they detested, a man whom they hated, stands up there and preaches the Gospel, and three thousand of them are immediately convicted and converted, and become disciples of the Lord Jesus Christ, and are willing to lay down their lives for the Son of God. It may have been on that occasion that Stephen was converted, the first martyr, and some of the men who soon after gave up their lives for Christ. This seems to me the greatest miracle this world has ever seen. But Peter did not labor alone; the Spirit of God was with him; hence the marvelous results.

The Jewish law required that there should be two witnesses, and so we find that when Peter preached there was a second witness. Peter testified of Christ, and Christ says when the Holy Spirit comes He will testify of Me. And they both bore witness to the verities of our Lord's incarnation, ministry, death, and resurrection, and the result was that a multitude turned as with one heart unto the Lord. Our failure now is, that preachers ignore the Cross, and veil Christ with sapless sermons and superfine language. They don't just present Him to the people plainly, and that is why, I believe, that the Spirit of God don't work with power in our churches.

What we need is to preach Christ and present Him to a perishing world. The world can get on very well without you and me, but the world can not get on without Christ, and therefore we must testify of Him, and the world, I believe, today is just hungering and thirsting for this divine, satisfying portion. Thousands and thousands are sitting in darkness, knowing not of this great Light, but when we begin to preach Christ honestly, faithfully, sincerely and truthfully; holding Him up, not ourselves; exalting Christ and not our theories; presenting Christ and not our opinions; advocating Christ and not some false doctrine; then the Holy Ghost will come and bear witness. He will testify that what we say is true. When He comes He will confirm the Word with signs following. This is one of the strongest proofs that our Gospel is Divine; that it is of Divine origin; that not only did Christ teach these things, but when leaving the world He said, "He shall glorify Me," and "He will testify of Me." If you will just look at the second chapter of Acts — to that wonderful sermon that Peter preached — the thirty-sixth verse, you read these words: "Therefore let all the house of Israel know assuredly that God hath made that same Jesus whom ye crucified, both Lord and Christ." And when Peter said this the Holy Ghost descended upon the people and testified of Christ — bore witness in signal demonstration that all this was true.

And again, in the fortieth verse, "And with many other words did He testify and exhort, saying, Save yourselves from this untoward generation." With many other words did He testify, not only these words that have been recorded, but many other words.

THE SURE GUIDE

Turn to the sixteenth chapter of John, in the thirteenth verse, and read: "Howbeit, when He, the Spirit of Truth is come, He will guide you into all truth; for He shall not speak of Himself; but whatsoever He shall hear that shall He speak; and He will show you things to come." He will guide you into all truth. Now there is not a truth that we ought to know but the Spirit of God will guide us into it if we will let Him; if we will yield ourselves up to be directed by the Spirit, and let Him lead us, He will guide us into all truth. It would have saved us from a great many dark hours if we had only been willing to let the Spirit of God be our counsellor and guide.

Lot never would have gone to Sodom if he had been guided by the Spirit of God. David never would have fallen into sin and had all that trouble with his family if he had been guided by the Spirit of God.

There are many Lots and Davids now-a-day. The churches are full of them. Men and women are in total darkness, because they have not been willing to be guided by the Spirit of God. "He shall guide you into all truth. He shall not speak of Himself." He shall speak of the ascended glorified Christ.

What would be thought of a messenger, entrusted by an absent husband with a message for his wife or mother who, on arrival, only talked of himself, and his conceits, and ignored both the husband and the message? You would simply call it outrageous. What then must be the crime of the professed teacher who speaks of himself, or some insipid theory, leaving out Christ and His Gospel? If we witness according to the Spirit, we must witness of Jesus.

The Holy Spirit is down here in this dark world to just speak of the Absent One, and He takes the things of Christ and brings them to our mind. He testifies of Christ; He guides us into the truth about Him.

RAPPINGS IN THE DARK

I want to say right here, that I think in this day a great many children of God are turning aside and committing a grievous sin. I don't know as they think it is a sin, but if we examine the Scriptures, I am sure we will find that it is a great sin. We are told that the Comforter is sent into the world to "guide us into all truth," and if He is sent for that purpose, do we need any other guide?

Need we hide in the darkness, consulting with mediums, who profess to call up the spirits of the dead? Do you know what the Word of God pronounces against that fearful sin? I believe it is one of the greatest sins we have to contend with at the present day. It is dishonoring to the Holy Spirit for me to go and summon up the dead and confer with them, even if it were possible.

I would like you to notice the 10th chapter of 1st Chronicles, and 13th verse:

> "So Saul died for his transgression which he had committed against the Lord, even against the Word of the Lord, which he kept not, and also for asking counsel of one that had a familiar spirit, to inquire of it; and inquired not of the Lord: therefore He slew him, and turned the kingdom unto David the son of Jesse."

God slew him for this very sin. Of the two sins that are brought against Saul here, one is that he would not listen to the Word of God, and the second is that he consulted a familiar spirit. He was snared by this great evil, and sinned against God.

Saul fell right here, and there are a great many of God's professed children today who think there is no harm in consulting a medium who pretends to call up some of the departed to inquire of them.

But how dishonoring it is to God who has sent the Holy Spirit into this world to guide us "into all truth." There is not a thing that I need to know, there is not a thing that is important for me to know; there is not a thing that I ought to know but the Spirit of God will reveal it to me through the Word of God, and if I turn my back upon the Holy Spirit, I am dishonoring the Spirit of God, and I am committing a grievous sin. You know we read in Luke, where that rich man in the other world wanted to have some one sent to his father's house to warn his five brothers, Christ said They have Moses and the prophets, and if they will not hear them, they will not hear one though he rose from the dead. Moses and the prophets, the part of the Bible then completed, that is enough. But a great many people now want something besides the Word of God, and are turning aside to these false lights.

SPIRITS THAT PEEP AND MUTTER

There is another passage which reads, "And when they shall

say unto you, seek unto them that have familiar spirits, and unto wizards that peep and mutter: Should not a people seek unto their God? for the living to the dead?" What is that but table-rapping, and cabinet-hiding? If it was a message from God, do you think you would have to go into a dark room and put out all the lights? In secret my Master taught nothing. God is not in that movement, and what we want, as children of God, is to keep ourselves from this evil. And then notice, the verse following, quoted so often out of its connection. "To the law and to the testimony; if they speak not according to this word, it is because there is no light in them." Any man, any woman, who comes to us with any doctrine that is not according to the law and the testimony, let us understand that they are from the evil one, and that they are enemies of righteousness. They have no light in them. Now you will find these people who are consulting familiar spirits, first and last, attack the Word of God. They don't believe it. Still a great many people say, you must hear both sides — but if a man should write me a most slanderous letter about my wife, I don't think I would have to read it; I should tear it up and throw it to the winds. Have I to read all the infidel books that are written, to hear both sides? Have I to take up a book that is a slander on my Lord and Master, who has redeemed me with His blood? Ten thousand times No; I will not touch it.

"Now the Spirit speaketh expressly, that in the latter times some shall depart from the faith, giving heed to seducing spirits, and doctrines of devils." (1 Tim., 4:1) That is pretty plain language, isn't it? "Doctrines of devils." Again, "speaking lies in hypocrisy; having their consciences seared with a hot iron." There are other passages of Scripture warning against every delusion of Satan. Let us ever remember the Spirit has been sent into the world to guide us into all truth. We don't want any other guide; He is enough. Some people say, "Is not conscience a safer guide than the Word and the Spirit?" No, it is not. Some people don't seem to have any conscience, and don't know what it means. Their education has a good deal to do with conscience. There are persons who will say that their conscience did not tell them that they had done wrong until after the wrong was done; but what we want, is something to tell us a thing is wrong before we do it. Very often a man will go and commit some awful crime, and after it is done his conscience will wake up and lash and scourge him, and then it is too late, the act is done.

THE UNERRING GUIDE

I am told by people who have been over the Alps, that the guide fastens them, if they are going in a dangerous place, right to himself, and he just goes on before; they are fastened to the guide.

And so should the Christian be linked to His unerring Guide, and be safely upheld. Why, if a man was going through the Mammoth Cave, it would be death to him if he strayed away from his guide — if separated from him, he would certainly perish; there are pitfalls in that cave and a bottomless river, and there would be no chance for a man to find his way through that cave without a guide or a light. So there is no chance for us to get through the dark wilderness of this world alone. It is folly for a man or woman to think that they can get through this evil world without the light of God's Word and the guidance of the Divine Spirit. God sent Him to guide us through this great journey, and if we seek to work independent of Him, we shall stumble into the deep darkness of eternity's night.

But bear in mind the Words of the Spirit of God; if you want to be guided, you must study the Word; because the Word is the light of the Spirit. In the 14th chapter of John and 26th verse, we read:

> "But the Comforter, which is the Holy Ghost, whom the Father will send in my name, He shall teach you all things, and bring all things to your remembrance, whatsoever I have said unto you."

Again in John 14:13:

> "Howbeit when He, the Spirit of Truth is come, He will guide you into all truth: for He shall not speak of Himself; but whatsoever He shall hear, that shall He speak: and He will show you things to come."

"He will show you things to come." A great many people seem to think that the Bible is out of date, that it is an old book, and they think it has passed its day. They say it was very good for the dark ages, and that there is some very good history in it; but then it was not intended for the present time; that we are living in a very enlightened age, and that men can get on very well without the old book; that we have outgrown it. They think we have no use for it, because it is an old book. Now you might just as well say that the sun, which has shone so long, is now so old that it is out of date, and that whenever a man builds a house he need not put any windows in it, because we have got a newer light and a better light; we have gaslight and this new electric light. These are something new; and I would advise people, if they think the Bible is too old and worn out, when they build houses, not to put any windows in them, but just to light them with this new electric light; that is something new, and this is what they are anxious for.

People talk about this Book as if they understood it; but we don't know much about it yet. The press gives us the daily news of what has taken place. This Bible, however, tells us what is about to take place. This is new; we have the news here in this Book; this tells us of the things that will surely come to pass; and that is a great deal newer than anything in the newspapers. It tells us that the Spirit shall teach us all things; not only guide us into all truth, but teach us all things; He teaches us how to pray, and I don't think there has ever been a prayer upon this sin-cursed earth that has been indicted by the Holy Spirit but was answered. There is much praying that is not indicted by the Holy Spirit. In former years I was very ambitious to get rich; I used to pray for one hundred thousand dollars; that was my aim, and I used to say, "God does not answer my prayer; He does not make me rich." But I had no warrant for such a prayer; yet a good many people pray in that way; they think that they pray, but they do not pray according to the Scriptures. The Spirit of God has nothing to do with their prayers, and such prayers are not the product of His teaching.

It is the Spirit who teaches us how to answer our enemies. If a man strikes me, I should not pull out a revolver and shoot him. The Spirit of the Lord don't teach me revenge; He don't teach me that it is necessary to draw the sword and cut a man down in order to defend my rights. Some people say, You are a coward if you don't strike back. Christ says, turn the other cheek to him who smites. I would rather take Christ's teaching than any other. I don't think a man gains much by loading himself down with weapons to defend himself. There has been life enough sacrificed in this country to teach men a lesson in this regard. The Word of God is a much better protection than the revolver. We had better take the Word of God to protect us, by accepting its teaching, and living out its precepts.

AN AID TO MEMORY

It is a great comfort to us to remember that another office of the Spirit is to bring the teaching of Jesus to our remembrance. This was our Lord's promise, "He shall teach you all things, and bring all things to your remembrance."(Jn. 14:26)

How striking that is. I think there are many Christians who have had that experience. They have been testifying, and found that while talking for Christ the Spirit has just brought into mind some of the sayings of the Lord Jesus Christ, and their mind was soon filled with the Word of God. When we have the Spirit resting upon us, we can speak with authority and power, and the Lord will bless our testimony and bless our work. I believe the reason why God makes use of so few in the Church, is because there is not in them the power that God can use. He is not going to use our ideas, but we must have the Word of God hid in our hearts, and then, the Holy Spirit inflaming us, we will have the testimony which will be rich, and sweet, and fresh, and the Lord's Word will vindicate itself in blessed results. God wants to use us; God wants to make us channels of blessing; but we are in such a condition He does not use us. That is the trouble; there are so many men who have no testimony for the Lord; if they speak, they speak without saying anything, and if they pray, their prayer is powerless; they do not plead in prayer; their prayer is just a few set phrases that you have heard too often. Now what we want, is to be so full of the Word, that the Spirit coming upon us shall bring to mind — bring to our remembrance — the words of the Lord Jesus.

In 1 Cor. 2:9, it is written:

> "Eye hath not seen, nor ear heard, neither have entered into the heart of man the things which God hath prepared for them that love Him."

We hear that quoted so often in prayer — many a man weaves it into his prayer and stops right there. And the moment you talk about Heaven, they say, "Oh, we don't know anything about Heaven it hath not entered into the heart of man; eye hath not seen; it is all speculation; we have nothing to do with it; and they say they quote it as it is written." "Eye hath not seen, nor ear heard; neither have entered into the heart of man the things which God hath prepared for them that love Him." What next — "but God hath revealed them unto us by His Spirit." You see the Lord hath revealed them unto us: "For the Spirit searches all things — yea, the deep things of God." That is just what the Spirit does.

LONG AND SHORT SIGHT

He brings to our mind what God has in store for us. I heard a man, some time ago, speaking about Abraham. He said "Abraham was not tempted by the well-watered plains of Sodom, for Abraham was what you might call a long-sighted man; he had his eyes set on the city which had foundation — 'whose Builder and Maker is God.'" But Lot was a short-sighted man; and there are many people in the Church who are very short-sighted; they only see things right around them they think good. Abraham was long-sighted; he had glimpses of the celestial city. Moses was long-sighted, and he left the palaces of Egypt and identified himself with God's people — poor people, who were slaves; but he had something in view yonder; he could see something God had in store. Again there are some people who are sort of long-sighted and shortsighted, too.

I have a friend who has one eye that is long-sighted and the other is short-sighted; and I think the Church is full of this kind of people. They want one eye for the world and the other for the Kingdom of God. Therefore, everything, is blurred, one eye is long and the other is short, all is confusion, and they "see men as trees walking." The Church is filled with that sort of people. But Stephen was long-sighted; he looked clear into heaven; they couldn't convince him even when he was dying, that Christ had not ascended to heaven. "Look, look yonder," he says, "see Him over there; He is on the throne, standing at the right hand of God;" and he looked clear into heaven; the world had no temptation for him; he had put the world under his feet. Paul was another of those long-sighted men; he had been caught up and seen things unlawful for him to utter; things grand and glorious.

I tell you when the Spirit of God is on us the world looks very empty; the world has a very small hold upon us, and we begin to let go our hold of it. When the Spirit of God is on us we will just let go the things of time and lay hold of things eternal. This is the Church's need today; we want the Spirit to come in mighty power, and consume all the vile dross there is in us. Oh! that the Spirit of fire may come down and burn everything in us that is contrary to God's blessed Word and Will.

In John 14:16, we read of the Comforter. This is the first time He is spoken of as the Comforter. Christ had been their Comforter. God had sent Him to comfort the sorrowing. It was prophesied of Him, "The Spirit of the Lord is upon me, because He hath anointed me to preach the Gospel to the poor; He has sent me to heal the broken-hearted." You can't heal the brokenhearted without the Comforter; but the world would not have the first Comforter, and so they rose up and took Him to Calvary and put him to death; but on going away He said, "I will send you another Comforter; you shall not be comfortless; be of good cheer, little flock; it is the Father's good pleasure to give you the kingdom." All these sweet passages are brought to the remembrance of God's people, and they help us to rise out of the fog and mist of this world. O, what a comforter is the Holy Spirit of God!

THE FAITHFUL FRIEND

The Holy Spirit tells a man of his faults in order to lead him to a better life. In John 16:8, we read: "He is to reprove the world of sin." Now, there are a class of people who don't like this part of the Spirit's work. Do you know why? Because He convicts them of sin; they don't like that. What they want is some one to speak comforting words and make everything pleasant; keep everything all quiet; tell them there is peace when there is war; tell them it is light when it is dark, and tell them everything is growing better; that the world is getting on amazingly in goodness; that it is growing better all the time; that is the kind of preaching they seek for. Men think they are a great deal better than their fathers were. That suits human nature, for it is full of pride. Men will strut around and say, "Yes, I believe that; the world is improving; I am a good deal better man than father was; my father was too strict; he was one of those old Puritanical men who was so rigid. O, we are getting on; we are more liberal; my father wouldn't think of going out riding on Sunday, but we will; we will trample the laws of God under our feet; we are better than our fathers."

That is the kind of preaching which some dearly love, and there are preachers who tickle such itching ears. When you bring the Word of God to bear upon them, and when the Spirit drives it home, then men will say: "I don't like that kind of preaching; I will never go to hear that man again;" and sometimes they will get up and stamp their way out of church before the speaker gets through; they don't like it. But when the Spirit of God is at work he convicts men of sin. "When He comes He will reprove the world of sin, of righteousness and of judgment; of sin" — not because men swear and lie and steal and get drunk and murder — "of sin because they believe not on Me."

THE CLIMAX SIN

That is the sin of the world. Why, a great many people think that unbelief is a sort of misfortune, but do not know, if you will allow me the expression, it is the damning sin of the world today; that is what unbelief is, the mother of all sin. There would not be a drunkard walking the streets, if it were not for unbelief; there would not be a harlot walking the streets, if it were not for unbelief; there would not be a murderer, if it was not for unbelief; it is the germ of all sin. Don't think for a moment that it is a misfortune, but just bear in mind it is an awful sin, and may the Holy Spirit convict every reader that unbelief is making God a liar. Many a man has been knocked down on the streets because some one has told him he was a liar. Unbelief is giving God the lie; that is the plain English of it. Some people seem to boast of their unbelief; they seem to think it is quite respectable to be an infidel and doubt God's Word, and they will vainly boast and say, "I have intellectual difficulties; I can't believe." Oh that the Spirit of God may come and convict men of sin! That is what we need — His convicting power, and I am so thankful that God has not put that into our hands. We have not to convict men; if we had I would get discouraged, and give up preaching, and go back to business within the next forty-eight hours. It is my work to preach and hold up the Cross and testify of Christ; but it is His work to convict men of sin and lead them to Christ.

One thing I have noticed, that some conversions don't amount to anything; that if a man professes to be converted without conviction of sin, he is one of those stony-ground hearers who don't bring forth much fruit. The first little wave of persecution, the first breath of opposition, and the man is back in the world again. Let us pray, dear Christian reader, that God may carry on a deep and thorough work, that men may be convicted of sin so that they can not rest in unbelief. Let us pray God it may be a thorough work in the land. I would a great deal rather see a hundred men thoroughly converted, truly born of God, than to see a thousand professed conversions where the Spirit of God has not convicted of sin.

Don't let us cry "Peace, peace, when there is no peace." Don't go to the man who is living in sin, and tell him all he has to do is to stand right up and profess, without any hatred for sin. Let us ask God first to show every man the plague of his own heart, that the Spirit, may convict them of sin. Then will the work in our hands be real, and deep, and abide the fiery trial which will try every man's labor.

Thus far, we have found the work of the Spirit is to impart life, to implant hope, to give liberty, to testify of Christ, to guide us into all truth, to teach us all things, to comfort the believers, and to convict the world of sin.

> "Holy Spirit, faithful guide,
> Ever near the Christian's side;
> Gently lead us by the hand,
> Pilgrims in a desert land;
> Weary souls for e'er rejoice,
> While they hear that sweetest voice,
> Whisp'ring softly, wanderer come!
> Follow Me, I'll guide thee home.
>
> Ever present, truest Friend,
> Ever near Thine aid to lend,
> Leave us not to doubt and fear,
> Groping on in darkness drear,
> When the storms are raging sore,
> Hearts grow faint, and hopes give o'er;
> Whisp'ring softly, wanderer come!

Follow Me, I'll guide thee home.

When our days of toil shall cease,
Waiting still for sweet release,
Nothing left but heaven and prayer,
Wond'ring if our names were there,
Wading deep the dismal flood,
Pleading nought but Jesus' blood;
Whisp'ring softly, wanderer come!
Follow Me, I'll guide thee home."

"Oh! Spirit of God, whose voice I hear,
Sweeter than sweetest music, appealing
In tones of tenderness and love;
Whose comforts delight my soul, and
Fills the temple of my heart with joy beyond compare.
I need Thee day by day, and each day's moment, Lord.
I sigh for greater likeness
To Him who loved me unto death, and loves me still.
'Tis Thine to lead me to Him; 'tis Thine to ope the eye,
To manifest His royal glories to my longing heart;
'Tis Thine the slumbering saint to waken
And discipline this blood-touched ear
To hearken to my heavenly Lover's voice,
And quickly speed His summons to obey.
Oh! Spirit of the Mighty God, uplift my faith
Till heaven's precious light shall flood my soul,
And the shining of my face declare
That I have seen the face of God."

CHAPTER 4

POWER IN OPERATION

> "Ye are not your own." "Your bodies are the temples of the Holy Ghost." Is that an unmeaning metaphor, or an over-worded expression? When the Holy Spirit enters the soul, heaven enters with Him. The heart is compared to a temple. God never enters without His attendants; repentance cleanses the house; faith provides for the house; watchfulness, like the porter, takes care of it; prayer is a lively messenger, learns what is wanted, and then goes for it; faith tells him where to go, and he never goes in vain; joy is the musician of this temple, tuning to the praises of God and the Lamb; and this terrestrial temple shall be removed to the celestial world, for the trumpet shall sound, and the dead shall be raised. — *Rowland Hill.*

The power we have been considering is the Presence of the Holy Spirit. He is omnipotent. Power in operation is the actions of the Spirit or the fruit of the Spirit. This we shall now consider. Paul writes in Gal. 5:16, etc.:

> "This I say then, walk in the Spirit, and ye shall not fulfill the lust of the flesh. For the flesh lusteth against the Spirit, and the Spirit against the flesh; and these are contrary, the one to the other; so that ye can not do the things that ye would. But if ye be led of the Spirit, ye are not under the law." * * * "But the fruit of the Spirit is love, joy, peace, long-suffering, gentleness, goodness, faith, meekness, temperance; against such there is no law. And they that are Christ's have crucified the flesh with the affections and lusts. If we live in the Spirit, let us also walk in the Spirit. Let us not be desirous of vainglory, provoking one another, envying one another."

Now there is a life of perfect peace, perfect joy, and perfect love, and that ought to be the aim of every child of God; that ought to be their standard; and they should not rest until having attained to that position. That is God's standard, where He wants all His children. These nine graces mentioned in this chapter in Galatians can be divided in this way: Love and peace and joy are all to God. God looks for that fruit from each one of His children, and that is the kind of fruit which is acceptable with Him. Without that we can not please God. He wants, above everything else that we possess, love, peace and joy. And then the next three — goodness, long-suffering and gentleness — are towards man. That is our outward life to those that we are coming in contact with continually — daily, hourly. The next three — faith, temperance, meekness — are in relation to ourselves; and in that way we can just take the three divisions, and it will be of some help to us.

The first thing that meets us as we enter the kingdom of God, you might say are these first three graces,

LOVE, PEACE, AND JOY

When a man who has been living in sin turns from his sins, and turns to God with all his heart, he is met on the threshold of the divine life by these sister graces. The love of God is shed abroad in his heart by the Holy Ghost. The peace of God comes at the same time, and also the joy of the Lord. We can all put the test to ourselves, if we have them. It is not anything that we can make. The great trouble with many is that they are trying to make these graces. They are trying to make love; they are trying to make peace; they are trying to make joy. But they are not creatures of human planting. To produce them of ourselves is impossible. That is an act of God. They come from above. It is God who speaks the word and gives the love; it is God who gives the peace; it is God who gives the joy, and we possess all by receiving Jesus Christ by faith into the heart; for when Christ comes by faith into the heart, then the Spirit is there, and if we have the Spirit, we will have the fruit.

If the whole Church of God could live as the Lord would have them live, why Christianity would be the mightiest power this world has ever seen. It is the low standard of Christian life that is causing so much trouble. There are a great many stunted Christians in the Church; their lives are stunted; they are like a tree planted in poor soil — the soil is hard and stony, and the roots can not find the rich loamy soil needed. Such believers have not grown in these sweet graces. Peter, in his second epistle, 1st chapter and 5th verse, writes:

"And besides this, giving all diligence, add to your faith virtue; and to virtue knowledge; and to knowledge temperance; and to temperance patience; and to patience, godliness; and to godliness, brotherly kindness; and to brotherly kindness, charity. For if these things be in you and abound, they make you that ye shall neither be barren nor unfruitful in the knowledge of our Lord Jesus Christ."

Now, if we have these things in us, I believe that we will be constantly bringing forth fruit that will be acceptable with God. It won't be just a little every now and then, when we spur ourselves up and work ourselves up into a certain state of mind or into an excited condition, and work a little while and then become cold, and discouraged, and disheartened, but we shall be neither unfruitful nor barren, bringing forth fruit constantly, we will grow in grace and be filled with the Spirit of God.

WHAT WINS

A great many parents have inquired of me how to win their children. They say they have talked with them, and sometimes they have scolded them and have lectured them, and signally failed. I think there is no way so sure to win our families and our neighbors, and those about whom we are anxious, to Christ, than just to adorn the doctrine of Jesus Christ in our lives, and grow in all these graces. If we have peace and joy and love and gentleness and goodness and temperance; not only being temperate in what we drink, but in what we eat, and temperate in our language, guarded in our expressions; if we just live in our homes as the Lord would have us, an even Christian life day by day, we shall have a quiet and silent power proceeding from us, that will constrain them to believe on the Lord Jesus Christ. But an uneven life, hot today and cold tomorrow, will only repel. Many are watching God's people. It is just the very worst thing that can happen to those whom we want to win to Christ, to see us, at any time, in a cold, backslidden state. This is not the normal condition of the Church; it is not God's intention; He would have us growing in all these graces, and the only true, happy, Christian life is to be growing, constantly growing in the love and favor of God, growing in all those delightful graces of the Spirit.

Even the vilest, the most impure, acknowledge the power of goodness; they recognize the fruit of the Spirit. It may condemn their lives and cause them to say bitter things at times, but down deep in their hearts they know that the man or woman who is living that kind of life, is superior to them. The world don't satisfy them, and if we can show the world that Jesus Christ does satisfy us in our present life, it will be more powerful than the eloquent words of professional reformers. A man may preach with the eloquence of an angel, but if he don't live what he preaches, and act out in his home and his business what he professes, his testimony goes for naught, and the people say it is all hypocrisy after all; it is all a sham. Words are very empty, if there is nothing back of them. Your testimony is poor and worthless, if there is not a record back of that testimony consistent with what you profess. What we need is to pray to God to lift us up out of this low, cold, formal state that we have been living in, that we may live in the atmosphere of God continually, and that the Lord may lift upon us the light of his countenance, and that we may shine in this world, reflecting His grace and glory.

The first of the graces spoken of in Galatians, and the last mentioned in Peter, is charity or love. We can not serve God, we can not work for God unless we have love. That is the key which unlocks the human heart. If I can prove to a man that I come to him out of pure love; if a mother shows by her actions that it is pure love that prompts her advising her boy to lead a different life, not a selfish love, but that it is for the glory of God, it won't be long before that mother's influence will be felt by that boy, and he will begin to think about this matter, because true love touches the heart quicker than anything else.

POWER OF LOVE

Love is the badge that Christ gave His disciples. Some put on one sort of badge and some another. Some put on a strange kind of dress, that they may be known as Christians, and some put on a crucifix, or something else, that they may be known as Christians. But love is the only badge by which the disciples of our Lord Jesus Christ are known. "By this shall all men know that ye are My disciples, if ye have love one toward another."

Therefore, though a man stand before an audience and speak with the eloquence of a Demosthenes, or of the greatest living orator, if there is no love back of his words, it is like sounding brass and a tinkling cymbal. I would recommend all Christians to read the thirteenth chapter of First Corinthians constantly, abiding in it day and night, not spending a night or a day there, but just go in there and spend all our time — summer and winter, twelve months in the year, then the power of Christ and Christianity would be felt as it never has been in the history of the world. See what this chapter says:

> "Though I speak with the tongues of men and of angels, and have not charity, I am become as sounding brass or a tinkling cymbal. And though I have the gift of prophecy, and understand all mysteries, and all knowledge; and though I have all faith, so that I could remove mountains, and have not charity, I am nothing."

A great many are praying for faith; they want extraordinary faith; they want remarkable faith. They forget that love exceeds faith. The Charity spoken of in the above verses, is Love, the fruit of the Spirit, the great motive-power of life. What the Church of God needs today is love — more love to God and more love to our fellow-men. If we love God more, we will love our fellow-men more. There is no doubt about that. I used to think that I should like to have lived in the days of the prophets; that I should like to have been one of the prophets, to prophesy, and to see the beauties of heaven and describe them to men; but, as I understand the Scriptures now, I would a good deal rather live in the thirteenth chapter of 1st Corinthians and have this love that Paul is speaking of, the love of God burning in my soul like an unquenchable flame, so that I may reach men and win them for heaven.

A man may have wonderful knowledge, that may unravel the mysteries of the Bible, and yet be as cold as an icicle. He may glisten like the snow in the sun. Sometimes you have wondered why it was that certain ministers who have had such wonderful magnetism, who have such a marvelous command of language, and who preach with such mental strength, haven't had more conversions. I believe, if the truth was known, you would find no divine love back of their words, no pure love in their sermons. You may preach like an angel, Paul says, "with the tongues of men and of angels," but if you have not love, it amounts to nothing. "And though I bestow all my goods to feed the poor," — a man may be very charitable, and give away all his goods; a man may give all he has, but if it is not the love of God which prompts the gift, it will not be acceptable with God. "And though I give my body to be burned, and have not charity" — have not love — "it profiteth me nothing." A man may go to the stake for his principles; he may go to the stake for what he believes, but if it is not love to God which actuates him, it will not be acceptable to God.

LOVE'S WONDERFUL EFFECTS

> "Charity suffereth long, and is kind; charity envieth not; charity vaunteth not itself, is not puffed up.
>
> Doth not behave itself unseemly, seeketh not her own, is not easily provoked, thinketh no evil."

That's the work of love. It is not easily provoked. Now if a man has no love of God in his heart, how easy it is to become offended; perhaps with the church because some members of the church don't treat him just right, or some men of the church don't bow to him on the street, he takes offense, and that is the last you see of him. Love is long-suffering. If I love the Lord Jesus Christ, these little things are not going to separate me from His people. They are like the dust in the balance. Nor will the cold, formal treatment of hypocrites in the church quench that love I have in my heart for Him. If this love is in the heart, and the fire is burning on the altar, we will not be all the time finding fault with other people and criticizing what they have done.

CRITICS BEWARE

Love will rebuke evil, but will not rejoice in it. Love will be impatient of sin, but patient with the sinner. To form the habit of finding fault constantly, is very damaging to spiritual life; it is about the lowest and meanest position that a man can take. I never saw a man who was aiming to do the best work, but there could have been some improvement; I never did anything in my life, I never addressed an audience, that I didn't think I could have done better, and I have often upbraided myself that I had not done better; but to sit down and find fault with other people when we are doing nothing ourselves, not lifting our hands to save some one, is all wrong, and is the opposite of holy, patient, divine love.

Love is forbearance; and what we want is to get this spirit of criticism and fault finding out of the Church and out of our hearts and let each one of us live as if we had to answer for ourselves, and not for the community, at the last day. If we are living according to the 13th chapter of Corinthians, we will not be all the time finding fault with other people. "Love suffereth long, and is kind." Love forgets itself, and don't dwell upon itself. The woman who came to Christ with that alabaster box, I venture to say, never thought of herself. Little did she know what an act she was performing. It was just her love for the Master. She forgot the surroundings, she forgot everything else that was there; she broke that box and poured the ointment upon Him, and filled the house with its odor. The act, as a memorial, has come down these 1800 years. It is right here — the perfume of that box is in the world today. That ointment was worth $40 or $50; no small sum of those days for a poor woman. Judas sold the Son of God for about $15 or $20. But what this woman gave to Christ was everything that she had, and she became so occupied with Jesus Christ that she didn't think what people were going to say. So when we act with a single eye for the glory of our Lord, not finding fault with everything about us, but doing what we can in the power of this love, then will our deeds for God speak, and the world will acknowledge that we have been with Jesus, and that this glorious love has been shed abroad in our hearts.

If we don't love the Church of God, I am afraid it won't do us much good; if we don't love the blessed Bible, it will not do us much good. What we want, then, is to have love for Christ, to have love for His word, and to have love for the Church of God, and when we have love, and are living in that spirit, we will not be in the spirit of finding fault and working mischief.

AFTER LOVE, WHAT?

After love comes peace. I have before remarked, a great many people are trying to make peace. But that has already been done. God has not left it for us to do; all that we have to do is to enter into it. It is a condition, and instead of our trying to make peace and to work for peace, we want to cease all that, and sweetly enter into peace.

If I discover a man in the cellar complaining because there is no light there, and because it is cold and damp, I say: "My friend, come up out of the cellar. There is a good warm sun up here, a beautiful spring day, and it is warm, it is cheerful and light; come up, and enjoy it." Would he reply, "O, no, sir; I am trying to see if I can make light down here; I am trying to work myself into a warm feeling." And there he is working away, and he has been at it for a whole week. I can imagine my reader smile; but you may be smiling at your own picture; for this is the condition of many whom I daily meet who are trying to do this very thing — they are trying to work themselves into peace and joyful feelings. Peace is a condition into which we enter; it is a state; and instead of our trying to make peace, let us believe what God's Word declares, that peace has already been made by the blood of the Cross. Christ has made peace for us, and now what He desires is that we believe it and enter into it.

Now, the only thing that can keep us from peace is sin. God turneth the way of the wicked upside down. There is no peace for the wicked, saith my God. They are like the troubled sea that can not rest, casting up filth and mire all the while; but peace with God by faith in Jesus Christ — peace through the knowledge of forgiven sin, is like a rock; the waters go dashing and surging past it, but it abides. When we find peace, we shall not find it on the ground of innate goodness; it comes from without ourselves, but into us. In the 16th chapter of John and the 33d verse we read: "These things have I spoken unto you, that in me ye might have peace." In me ye might have peace. Jesus Christ is the author of peace. He procured peace. His gospel is the gospel of peace. "Behold I bring you good tidings of great joy which shall be unto all people; for unto you is born this day in the city of David a Saviour," and then came that chorus from heaven "Glory to God in the highest; peace on earth." He brought peace. "In the world ye shall have tribulation, but be of good cheer, I have overcome the world."

How true that in the world we have tribulation. Are you in tribulation? Are you in trouble? Are you in sorrow? Remember this is our lot. Paul had tribulation, and others shared in grief. Nor shall we be exempt from trial. But within, peace may reign undisturbed. If sorrow is our lot, peace is our legacy. Jesus gives peace; and do you know there is a good deal of difference between His peace and our peace? Any one can disturb our peace, but they can't disturb His peace. That is the kind of peace He has left us. Nothing can offend those who trust in Christ.

NOT EASILY OFFENDED

In the 119th Psalm and the 165th verse, we find "Great peace have they who love Thy law; and nothing shall offend them." The study of God's Word will secure peace. You take those Christians who are rooted and grounded in the Word of God, and you find they have great peace; but it is these who don't study their Bible, and don't know their Bible, who are easily offended when some little trouble comes, or some little persecution, and their peace is all disturbed; just a little breath of opposition, and their peace is all gone.

Sometimes I am amazed to see how little it takes to drive all peace and comfort from some people. Some slandering tongue will readily blast it. But if we have the peace of God, the world can not take that from us. It can not give it; it can not destroy it. We have to get it from above the world; it is peace which Christ gives. "Great peace have they which love Thy law, and nothing shall offend them." Christ says "blessed is he, whosoever shall not be offended in Me." Now, if you will notice, wherever there is a Bible-taught Christian, one who has the Bible well marked, and daily feeds upon the Word by prayerful meditation, he will not be easily offended.

Such are the people who are growing and working all the while. But it is these people who never open their Bibles, these people who never study the Scriptures, who become offended, and are wondering why they are having such a hard time. They are the persons who tell you that Christianity is not what it has been recommended to them; that they have found it was not all that we claim it to be. The real trouble is, they have not done as the Lord has told them to do. They have neglected the Word of God. If they had been studying the Word of God, they would not be in that condition. If they had been studying the Word of God, they would not have wandered these years away from God, living on the husks of the world. But the trouble is, they have neglected to care for the new life; they haven't fed it, and the poor soul, being starved, sinks into weakness and decay, and is easily stumbled or offended.

I met a man who confessed his soul had fed on nothing for forty years. "Well," said I, "that is pretty hard for the soul — giving it nothing to feed on!" And that man is but a type of thousands and tens of thousands today; their poor souls are starving. This body that we inhabit for a day, and then leave, we take good care of; we feed it three times a day, and we clothe it, and take care of it, and deck it, and by and by it is going into the grave to be eaten up by the worms; but the inner man, that is to live on and on, and on forever, is lean and starved.

SWEET WORDS

In the 6th chapter of Numbers and 22d verse we read:

> "And the Lord spake unto Moses, saying: Speak unto Aaron and unto his sons, saying, on this wise ye shall bless the children of Israel, saying unto them: The Lord bless thee and keep thee. The Lord make His face shine upon thee, and be gracious unto thee.
> The Lord lift up His countenance upon thee, and give thee peace."

I think these are about as sweet verses as we find in the Old Testament. I marked them years ago in my Bible, and many times I have turned over and read them. "The Lord lift up His countenance upon thee, and give thee peace." They remind us of the loving words of Jesus to his troubled disciples, "Peace, be still." The Jewish salutation used to be, as a man went into a house, "Peace be upon this house," and as he left the house the host would say, "Go in peace."

Then again, in the 14th chapter of John and the 27th verse, Jesus said: "Peace I leave with you, my peace I give unto you; not as the world giveth give I unto you. Let not your heart be troubled, neither let it be afraid." This is the precious legacy of Jesus to all His followers. Every man, every woman, every child, who believes in Him, may share in this portion. Christ has willed it to them, and His peace is theirs.

This then is our Lord's purpose and promise. My peace I give unto you. I give it, and I am not going to take it away again; I am going to leave it to you. "Not as the world giveth, give I unto you.

Let not your heart be troubled, neither let it be afraid." But you know, when some men make their wills and deed away their property, there are some sharp, shrewd lawyers who will get hold of that will and break it all to pieces; they will go into court and break the will, and the jury will set the will aside, and the money goes into another channel. Now this will that Christ has made, neither devil nor man can break it. He has promised to give us peace, and there are thousands of witnesses who can say: "I have my part of that legacy. I have peace; I came to Him for peace, and I got it; I came to Him in darkness; I came to Him in trouble and sorrow; I was passing under a deep cloud of affliction, and I came to Him and He said, 'Peace, be still.' And from that hour peace reigned in my soul." Yes, many have proved the invitation true, "Come unto Me all ye that labor and are heavy laden, and I will give you rest." They found rest when they came. He is the author of rest, He is the author of peace, and no power can break that will; yea, unbelief may question it, but Jesus Christ rose to execute His own will, and it is in vain for man to contest it. Infidels and skeptics may tell us that it is all a myth, and that there isn't anything in it, and yet the glorious tidings is ever repeated, "Peace on earth, good will to man," and the poor and needy, the sad and sorrowful, are made partakers of it.

So, my reader, you need not wait for peace any longer. All you have to do is to enter into it today. You need not try to make peace. It is a false idea; you can not make it. Peace is already made by Jesus Christ, and is now declared unto you.

PEACE DECLARED

When France and England were at war, a French vessel had gone off on a long voyage, a whaling voyage; and when they came back, the crew were short of water, and being now near an English port, they wanted to get water; but they were afraid that they would be taken if they went into that port; and some people in the port saw them, saw their signal of distress, and sent word to them that they need not be afraid, that the war was over, and peace had been declared. But they couldn't make those sailors believe it, and they didn't dare to go into port, although they were out of water; but at last they made up their minds that they had better go in and surrender up their cargo and surrender up their lives to their enemies than to perish at sea without water; but when they got in, they found out that peace had been declared, and that what had been told them was true. So there are a great many people who don't believe the glad tidings that peace has been made. Jesus Christ made peace on the Cross. He satisfied the claims of the law; and this law which condemns you and me has been fulfilled by Jesus Christ. He has made peace, and now He wants us just to enjoy it, just to believe it. Nor is there a thing to hinder us from doing it, if we will. We can enter into that blessing now, and have perfect peace. The promise is: "Thou wilt keep him in perfect peace whose mind is stayed on Thee. Trust ye in the Lord forever, for in the Lord Jehovah is everlasting strength."

Now, as long as our mind is stayed on our dear selves, we will never have peace. Some people think more of themselves than of all the rest of the world. It is self in the morning, self at noon, and self at night. It is self when they wake up, and self when they go to bed; and they are all the time looking at themselves and thinking about themselves, instead of "looking unto Jesus." Faith is an outward look. Faith does not look within; it looks without. It is not what I think, nor what I feel, nor what I have done, but it is what Jesus Christ is and has done, and so we should trust in Him who is our strength, and whose strength will never fail. After Christ rose from the grave, three times, John tells us, He met His disciples and said unto them, "Peace be unto you." There is peace for the conscience through His blood, and peace for the heart in His love.

SECRET OF JOY

Remember, then, that love is power, and peace is power; but now I will call attention to another fruit of the Spirit, and this too is power — the grace of joy. It is the privilege, I believe, of every Christian to walk in the light, as God is in the light, and to have that peace which will be flowing unceasingly as we keep busy about His work. And it is our privilege to be full of the joy of the Lord. We read, that when Philip went down to Samaria and preached, there was great joy in the city. Why? Because they believed the glad tidings. And that is the natural order, joy in believing. When we believe the glad tidings, there comes a joy into our souls. Also we are told that our Lord sent the seventy out, and that they went forth preaching salvation in the name of Jesus Christ, and the result was that there were a great many who were blessed; and the seventy returned, it says, with great joy, and when they came back they said that the very devils were subject to them, through His name.

The Lord seemed to just correct them in this one thing when He said, "Rejoice not that the devils are subject to you, but rejoice that your names are written in heaven." There is assurance for you. They had something to rejoice in now. God don't ask us to rejoice over nothing, but He gives us some ground for our joy. What would you think of a man or woman who seemed very happy to-day and full of joy, and couldn't tell you what made them so? Suppose I should meet a man on the street, and he was so full of joy that he should get hold of both my hands and say, "Bless the Lord, I am so full of joy!" "What makes you so full of joy?" "Well, I don't know." "You don't know?" "No, I don't; but I am so joyful that I just want to get out of the flesh." "What makes you feel so joyful?" "Well, I don't know." Would we not think such a person unreasonable? But there are a great many people who feel — who want to feel — that they are Christians before they are Christians; they want the Christian's experience before they become Christians; they want to have the joy of the Lord before they receive Jesus Christ. But this is not the Gospel order. He brings joy when He comes, and we can not have joy apart from Him; there is no joy away from Him; He is the author of it, and we find our joy in Him.

JOY IS UNSELFISH

Now, there are three kinds of joy; there is the joy of one's own salvation. I thought, when I first tasted that, it was the most delicious joy I had ever known, and that I could never get beyond it. But I found, afterward, there was something more joyful than that, namely, the joy of the salvation of others. Oh, the privilege, the blessed privilege, to be used of God to win a soul to Christ, and to see a man or woman being led out of bondage by some act of ours toward them. To think that God should condescend to allow us to be co-workers with Him. It is the highest honor we can wear. It surpasses the joy of our own salvation, this joy of seeing others saved. And then John said, He had no greater joy than to see His disciples walking in the truth. Every man who has been the means of leading souls to Christ understands what that means. Young disciples, walk in the truth and you will have joy all the while.

I think there is a difference between happiness and joy. Happiness is caused by things which happen around me, and circumstances will mar it, but joy flows right on through trouble; joy flows on through the dark; joy flows in the night as well as in the day; joy flows all through persecution and opposition; it flows right along, for it is an unceasing fountain bubbling up in the heart; a secret spring which the world can't see and don't know anything about; but the Lord gives His people perpetual joy when they walk in obedience to Him.

This joy is fed by the Divine Word. Jeremiah says in chapter 15:16:

> "Thy words were found, and I did eat them; and Thy Word was unto me the joy and rejoicing of my heart; for I am called by Thy name, O Lord."

He ate the words, and what was the result? He said they were the joy and rejoicing of his heart. Now people should look for joy in the Word, and not in the world; they should look for the joy which the Scriptures furnish, and then go work in the vineyard; because a joy that don't send me out to some one else, a joy that don't impel me to go and help the poor drunkard, a joy that don't prompt me to visit the widow and the fatherless, a joy that don't cause me to go into the Mission Sunday-school or other Christian work, is not worth having, and is not from above; a joy that does not constrain me to go and work for the Master, is purely sentiment and not real joy.

JOY IN PERSECUTION

Then it says in Luke 6:22:

> "Blessed are ye when men shall hate you, and when they shall separate you from their company, and shall reproach you and cast out your name as evil, for the Son of Man's sake. Rejoice ye in that day and leap for joy, for behold your reward is great in heaven for in like manner did their fathers unto the prophets."

Christians do not receive their reward down here. We have to go right against the current of the world. We may be unpopular, and we may go right against many of our personal friends if we live godly in Christ Jesus; and at the same time, if we are persecuted for the Master's sake, We will have this joy bubbling up; it just comes right up in our hearts all the while — a joy that is unceasing — that flows right on. The world can not choke that fountain. If we have Christ in the heart, by and by the reward will come.

The longer I live the more I am convinced that godly men and women are not appreciated in our day. But their work will live after them, and there will be a greater work done after they are gone, by the influence of their lives, than when they were living. Daniel is doing a thousand times more than when he was living in Babylon. Abraham is doing more today than he did on the plain with his tent and altar. All these centuries he has been living, and so we read, "Blessed are the dead that die in the Lord, from henceforth; yea saith the Spirit, that they may rest from their labors, and their works do follow them." Let us set the streams running that shall flow on after we have gone. If we have today persecution and opposition, let us press forward, and our reward will be great by and by.

Oh! think of this; the Lord Jesus, the Maker of heaven and earth, who created the world, says, "Great shall be thy reward." He calls it great. If some friend should say it is great, it might be very small; but when the Lord, the great and mighty God, says it is great, what must it be? Oh! the reward that is in store for those who serve Him! We have this joy, if we serve Him. A man or woman is not fit to work for God who is cast down, because they go about their work with a tell-tale face. "The joy of the Lord is your strength." What we need today is a joyful church. A joyful church will make inroads upon the works of Satan, and we will see the Gospel going down into dark lanes and dark alleys, and into dark garrets and cellars, and we will see the drunkards reached and the gamblers and the harlots come pressing into the kingdom of God. It is this carrying a sad countenance, with so many wrinkles on our brows, that retards Christianity. Oh may there come great joy upon believers everywhere, that we may shout for joy and rejoice in God day and night. A joyful church — let us pray for that, that the Lord may make us joyful, and when we have joy, then we will have success; and if we don't have the reward we think we should have here, let us constantly remember the rewarding time will come hereafter.

Some one has said, if you had asked men in Abraham's day who their great man was, they would have said Enoch, and not Abraham. If you had asked in Moses' day who their great man was, they would not have said it was Moses; he was nothing, but it would have been Abraham. If you had asked in the days of Elijah or Daniel, it wouldn't have been Daniel or Elijah; they were nothing; but it would have been Moses. And in the days of Jesus Christ — if you had asked in the days of Jesus Christ about John the Baptist or the apostles, you would hear they were mean and contemptible in the sight of the world, and were looked upon with scorn and reproach; but see how mighty they have become. And so we will not be appreciated in our day, but we are to toil on and work on, possessing this joy all the while. And if we lack it, let us cry: "Restore unto me the joy of Thy salvation, and uphold me with Thy free Spirit; then will I teach transgressors Thy ways, and sinners shall be converted unto Thee."

Again, the 15th chapter of John, and 11th verse, reads:

> "These things have I spoken unto you, that my joy might remain in you, and that your joy might be full."

And in the 16th chapter and 22d verse:

> "And ye now therefore have sorrow; but I will see you again, and your heart shall rejoice, and your joy no man taketh from you."

I am so thankful that I have a joy that the world can not rob me of; I have a treasure that the world can not take from me; I have something that it is not in the power of man or devil to deprive me of, and that is the joy of the Lord. "No man taketh it from you." In the second century, they brought a martyr before a king, and the king wanted him to recant and give up Christ and Christianity, but the man spurned the proposition. But the king said: "If you don't do it, I will banish you." The man smiled and answered: "You can't banish me from Christ, for He says He will never leave me nor forsake me." The king got angry, and said: "Well, I will confiscate your property and take it all from you." And the man replied: "My treasures are laid up on high; you can not get them." The king became still more angry, and said: "I will kill you."

"Why," the man answered, "I have been dead forty years; I have been dead with Christ; dead to the world, and my life is hid with Christ in God, and you can not touch it." And so we can rejoice, because we are on resurrection ground, having risen with Christ. Let persecution and opposition come, we can rejoice continually, and remember that our reward is great, reserved for us unto the day when He who is our Life shall appear, and we shall appear with Him in glory.

"The Spirit, oh, sinner,
In mercy doth move
Thy heart, so long hardened,
Of sin to reprove;
Resist not the Spirit,
Nor longer delay;
God's gracious entreaties may end with today.

Oh, child of the kingdom,
From sin service cease;
Be filled with the Spirit,
With comfort and peace.
Oh, grieve not the Spirit,
Thy Teacher is He,
That Jesus, thy Saviour, may glorified be.

Defiled is the temple,
Its beauty laid low,
On God's holy altar
The embers faint glow,
By love yet rekindled,
A flame may be fanned;
Oh, quench not the Spirit, the Lord is at hand!"
— *P. P. Bliss.*

CHAPTER 5

POWER HINDERED

The strokes of the "Sword of the Spirit" alight only on the conscience, and its edge is anointed with a bairn to heal every wound it may inflict. — *Dr. J. Harris*.

Every vain thought and idle word, and every wicked deed, is like so many drops to quench the Spirit of God. Some quench Him with the lust of the flesh; some quench Him with cares of the mind; some quench Him with long delays, that is, not plying the motion when it cometh, but crossing the good thoughts with bad thoughts, and doing a thing when the Spirit saith not. The Spirit is often grieved before He be quenched. — *H. Smith*.

In times when vile men held the high places of the land, a roll of drums was employed to drown the martyr's voice, lest the testimony of truth from the scaffold should reach the ears of the people, — an illustration of how men deal with their own consciences, and seek to put to silence the truth-telling voice of the Holy Spirit. — *Arnot*.

Israel, we are told, limited the Holy One of Israel. They vexed and grieved the Holy Spirit, and rebelled against His authority, but there is a special sin against Him, which we may profitably consider. The first description of it is in Matthew 12 the 22d verse:

THE UNPARDONABLE SIN

"Then was brought unto Him one possessed with a devil, blind and dumb; and He healed him, insomuch that the blind and dumb both spake and saw. And all the people were amazed, and said, Is not this the son of David? But when the Pharisees heard it, they said, This fellow doth not cast out devils, but by Beelzebub the prince of the devils. And Jesus knew their thoughts, and said unto them, Every kingdom divided against itself is brought to desolation; and every city or house divided against itself shall not stand. And if Satan cast out Satan, he is divided against himself; how shall then his kingdom stand? And if I by Beelzebub cast out devils, by whom do your children cast them out? therefore they shall be your judges. But if I cast out devils by the Spirit of God, then the kingdom of God is come unto you. Or else how can one enter into a strong man's house, and spoil his goods, except he first bind the strong man? and then he will spoil his house. He that is not with me is against me; and he that gathereth not with me, scattereth abroad. Wherefore I say unto you, all manner of sin and blasphemy shall be forgiven unto men; but the blasphemy against the Holy Ghost shall not be forgiven unto men. And whosoever speaketh a word against the Son of man, it shall be forgiven him; but whosoever speaketh against the Holy Ghost, it shall not be forgiven him, neither in this world, neither in the world to come."

That is Matthew's account. Now let us read Mark's account in chapter 3:21, etc.:

"And when His friends heard of it, they went out to lay hold on Him, for they said: He (that is Christ) is beside Himself. And the scribes which came down from Jerusalem said, He hath Beelzebub, and by the prince of the devils casteth He out devils."

The word Beelzebub means the Lord of Filth. They charged the Lord Jesus with being possessed not only with an evil spirit, but with a filthy spirit.

"And He called them unto Him, and said unto them in parables, How can Satan cast out Satan? And if a kingdom be divided against itself, that kingdom can not stand. And if a house be divided against itself, that house can not stand. And if Satan rise up against himself, and be divided, he can not stand, but hath an end. No man can enter into a strong man's house, and spoil his goods, except he will first bind the strong man; and then he will spoil his house. Verily I say unto you, all sins shall be forgiven unto the sons of men, and blasphemies wherewith soever they shall blaspheme: But he that shall blaspheme against the Holy Ghost hath never forgiveness, but is in danger of eternal damnation."

Now, if it stopped there, we would be left perhaps in darkness, and we would not exactly understand what the sin against the Holy

Ghost is; but the next verse of this same chapter of Mark just throws light upon the whole matter, and we need not be in darkness another minute if we really want light; for observe, the verse reads: "Because they said, He hath an unclean spirit."

Now, I have met a good many atheists and skeptics and deists and infidels, both in this country and abroad, but I never in my life met a man or woman who ever said that Jesus Christ was possessed of an unclean devil. Did you? I don't think you ever met such a person. I have heard men say bitter things against Christ, but I never heard any man stand up and say that he thought Jesus Christ was possessed with the devil, and that he cast out devils by the power of the devil; and I don't believe any man or woman has any right to say they have committed the unpardonable sin, unless they have maliciously, and willfully and deliberately said that they believe that Jesus Christ had a devil in Him, and that He was under the power of the devil, and that He cast out devils by the power of the devil. Because you perhaps have heard some one say that there is such a thing as grieving the Spirit of God, and resisting the Spirit of God until He has taken His flight and left you, then you have said "That is the unpardonable sin."

WHAT IT IS NOT

I admit there is such a thing as resisting the Spirit of God, and resisting till the Spirit of God has departed; but if the Spirit of God has left any, they will not be troubled about their sins. The very fact that they are troubled, shows that the Spirit of God has not left them. If a man is troubled about his sins, it is the work of the Spirit; for Satan never yet told him he was a sinner. Satan makes us believe that we are pretty good; that we are good enough without God, safe without Christ, and that we don't need salvation. But when a man wakes up to the fact that he is lost, that he is a sinner, that is the work of the Spirit; and if the Spirit of God had left him, he would not be in that state; and just because men and women want to be Christians, is a sign that the Spirit of God is drawing them.

If resisting the Spirit of God is an unpardonable sin, then we have all committed it, and there is no hope for any of us; for I do not believe there is a minister, or a worker in Christ's vineyard, who has not, some time in his life, resisted the Holy Ghost; who has not some time in his life rejected the Spirit of God. To resist the Holy Ghost is one thing, and to commit that awful sin of blasphemy against the Holy Ghost, is another thing; and we want to take the Scripture and just compare them.

Now, some people say, "I have such blasphemous thoughts; there are some awful thoughts that come into my mind against God," and they think that is the unpardonable sin. We are not to blame for having BAD THOUGHTS come into our minds. If we harbor them, then we are to blame. But if the devil comes and darts an evil thought into my mind, and I say, "Lord help me," sin is not reckoned to me. Who has not had evil thoughts come into his mind, flash into his heart, and been called to fight them!

One old divine says, "You are not to blame for the birds that fly over your head, but if you allow them to come down and make a nest in your hair, then you are to blame. You are to blame if you don't fight them off." And so with these evil thoughts that come flashing into our minds; we have to fight them, we are not to harbor them; we are not to entertain them. If I have evil thoughts come into my mind, and evil desires, it is no sign that I have committed the unpardonable sin. If I love these thoughts and harbor them, and think evil of God, and think Jesus Christ a blasphemer, I am responsible for such gross iniquity; but if I charge Him with being the prince of devils, then I am committing the unpardonable sin.

THE FAITHFUL FRIEND

Let us now consider the sin of "Grieving the Spirit." Resisting the Holy Ghost is one thing, grieving Him is another. Stephen charged the unbelieving Jews in the 7th chapter of Acts, "Ye do always resist the Holy Ghost as your fathers did, so do ye." The world has always been resisting the Spirit of God in all ages. That is the history of the world. The world is today resisting the Holy Spirit.

"Faithful are the wounds of a friend." The Divine Spirit as a friend reveals to this poor world its faults, and the world only hates Him for it. He shows them the plague of their hearts. He convinces or convicts them of sin, therefore they fight the Spirit of God. I believe there is many a man resisting the Holy Ghost; I believe there is many a man today fighting against the Spirit of God.

In the 4th chapter of Ephesians, in the 30th, 31st, and 32d verses, we read:

> "And grieve not the Holy Spirit of God, whereby ye are sealed unto the day of redemption. Let all bitterness, and wrath, and anger, and clamor, and evil speaking be put away from you, with all malice. And be ye kind, one to another, tender-hearted, forgiving one another, even as God for Christ's sake hath forgiven you."

Now, mark you, that was written to the Church at Ephesus. "Grieve not the Holy Spirit, whereby ye are sealed unto the day of redemption." I believe today the Church all over Christendom is guilty of grieving the Holy Spirit. There are a good many believers in different churches wondering why the work of God is not revived.

THE CHURCH GRIEVES THE SPIRIT

I think that if we search, we will find something in the Church grieving the Spirit of God; it may be a mere schism in the church; it may be some unsound doctrine; it may be some division in the Church. There is one thing I have noticed as I have traveled in different countries; I never yet have known the Spirit of God to work where the Lord's people were divided. There is one thing that we must have if we are to have the Holy Spirit of God to work in our midst, and that is unity. If a church is divided, the members should immediately seek unity. Let the believers come together and get the difficulty out of the way. If the minister of a church can not unite the people, if those that were dissatisfied will not fall in, it would be better for that minister to retire. I think there are a good many ministers in this country who are losing their time; they have lost, some of them, months and years; they have not seen any fruit, and they will not see any fruit, because they have a divided church. Such a church can not grow in divine things. The Spirit of God don't work where there is division, and what we want today is the spirit of unity among God's children, so that the Lord may work.

WORLDLY AMUSEMENTS

Then, another thing, I think, that grieves the Spirit, is the miserable policy of introducing questionable entertainments. There are the lotteries, for instance, that we have in many churches. If a man wants to gamble, he doesn't have to go to some gambling den; he can stay in the church. And there are fairs — bazaars, as they call them — where they have rafflings and grab-bags. And if he wants to see a drama, he don't need to go to the theater, for many of our churches are turned into theaters; he may stay right in the church and witness the acting. I believe all these things grieve the Spirit of God. I believe when we bring the Church down to the level of the world to reach the world, we are losing all the while and grieving the Spirit of God.

But some say, if we take that standard and lift it up high, it will drive away a great many members from our churches. I believe it, and I think the quicker they are gone the better. The world has come into the Church like a flood, and how often you find an ungodly choir employed to do the singing for the whole congregation; the idea that we need an ungodly man to sing praises to God! It was not long ago I heard of a church where they had an unconverted choir, and the minister saw something about the choir that he didn't like, and he spoke to the chorister, but the chorister replied: "You attend to your end of the church, and I will attend to mine." You can not expect the Spirit of God to work in a church in such a state as that.

UNCONVERTED CHOIRS

Paul tells us not to speak in an unknown tongue, and if we have choirs who are singing in an unknown tongue, why is not that just as great an abomination? I have been in churches where they have had a choir, who would rise and sing, and sing, and it seemed as if they sung five or ten minutes, and I could not understand one solitary word they sung, and all the while the people were looking around carelessly. There are, perhaps, a select few, very fond of fine music, and they want to bring the opera right into the church, and so they have opera music in the church, and the people, who are drowsy and sleepy, don't take part in the singing. They hire ungodly men, unconverted men, and these men will sometimes get the Sunday paper, and get back in the organ loft, and the moment the minister begins his sermon, they will take out their papers and read them all the while that the minister is preaching. The organist, provided he does not go out for a walk — if he happens to keep awake, will read his paper, or, perhaps, a novel, while the minister is preaching; and the minister wonders why God don't revive His work; he wonders why he is losing his hold on the congregation; he wonders why people don't come crowding into the church; why people are running after the world instead of coming into the church.

The trouble is that we have let down the standard; we have grieved the Spirit of God. One movement of God's power is worth more than all our artificial power, and what the Church of God wants today is to get down in the dust of humiliation and confession of sin, and go out and be separated from the world; and then see if we do not have power with God and with man.

WHAT IS SUCCESS?

The Gospel has not lost its power; it is just as powerful today as it ever has been. We don't want any new doctrine. It is still the old Gospel with the old power, the Holy Ghost power; and if the churches will but confess their sins and put them away, and lift the standard instead of pulling it down, and pray to God to lift us all up into a higher and holier life, then the fear of the Lord will come upon the people around us.

It was when Jacob put away strange gods and set his face toward Bethel that the fear of God fell upon the nations around. And when the churches turn towards God, and we cease grieving the Spirit, so that He may work through us, we will then have conversions all the while. Believers will be added to the Church daily. It is sad when you look over Christendom and see how desolate it is, and see how little spiritual life, spiritual power, there is in the Church of God today, many of the church members not even wanting this Holy Ghost power. They don't desire it; they want intellectual power; they want to get some man who will just draw a crowd; and a choir that will draw; not caring whether any one is saved. With them that is not the question. Only fill the pews, have good society, fashionable people, and dancing; such persons are found one night at the theater and the next night at the opera. They don't like the prayer-meetings; they abominate them; if the minister will only lecture and entertain, that would suit them.

I said to a man some time ago, "How are you getting on at your church?" "Oh, splendid." "Many conversions?" "Well — well, on that side we are not getting on so well. But," he said, "we rented all our pews and are able to pay all our running expenses; we are getting on splendidly." That is what the godless call "getting on splendidly;" because they rent the pews, pay the minister, and pay all the running expenses. Conversions! that is a strange thing. There was a man being shown through one of the cathedrals of Europe; he had come in from the country, and one of the men belonging to the cathedral was showing him around, when he inquired, "Do you have many conversions here?" "Many what?" "Many conversions here?" "Ah, man, this is not a Wesleyan chapel." The idea of there being conversions there! And you can go into a good many churches in this country and ask if they have many conversions there, and they would not know what it meant, they are so far away from the Lord; they are not looking for conversions, and don't expect them.

SHIPWRECKS

Alas! how many young converts have made shipwreck against such churches. Instead of being a harbor of delight to them, they have proved false lights, alluring them to destruction. Isn't it time for us to get down on our faces before God and cry mightily to Him to forgive us our sins. The quicker we own it the better. You may be invited to a party, and it may be made up of church members, and what will be the conversation? Oh, I got so sick of such parties that I left years ago; I would not think of spending a night that way; it is a waste of time; there is hardly a chance to say a word for the Master. If you talk of a personal Christ, your company becomes offensive; they don't like it; they want you to talk about the world, about a popular minister, a popular church, a good organ, a good choir, and they say, "Oh, we have a grand organ, and a superb choir," and all that, and it suits them; but that don't warm the Christian heart. When you speak of a risen Christ and a personal Saviour, they don't like it; the fact is, the world has come into the church and taken possession of it, and what we want to do is to wake up and ask God to forgive us for "Grieving the Spirit."

Dear reader, search your heart and inquire, Have I done anything to grieve the Spirit of God? If you have, may God show it to you today; if you have done any thing to grieve the Spirit of God, you want to know it today, and get down on your face before God and ask Him to forgive you and help you to put it away. I have lived long enough to know that if I can not have the power of the Spirit of God on me to help me to work for Him, I would rather die, than live just for the sake of living. How many are there in the church today, who have been members for fifteen or twenty years, but have never done a solitary thing for Jesus Christ? They can not lay their hands upon one solitary soul who has been blessed through their influence; they can not point today to one single person who has ever been lifted up by them.

QUENCH NOT

In 1st Thessalonians, 5th chapter, we are told not to Quench the Spirit. Now, I am confident the cares of the world are coming in and quenching the Spirit with a great many. They say: "I don't care for the world;" perhaps not the pleasures of the world so much after all as the cares of this life; but they have just let the cares come in and quench the Spirit of God. Anything that comes between me and God — between my soul and God — quenches the Spirit. It may be my family. You may say: "Is there any danger of my loving my family too much?" Not if we love God more; but God must have the first place. If I love my family more than God, then I am quenching the Spirit of God within me; if I love wealth, if I love fame, if I love honor, if I love position, if I love pleasure, if I love self, more than I love God who created and saved me, then I am committing a sin; I am not only grieving the Spirit of God, but quenching Him, and robbing my soul of His power.

EMBLEMS OF THE SPIRIT

But I would further call attention to the emblems of the Holy Spirit. An emblem is something that represents an object; the same as a balance is an emblem of justice, and a crown an emblem of royalty, and a scepter is an emblem of power; so we find in the 17th chapter of Exodus and 6th verse, that water is an emblem of the Holy Spirit. You find in the Smitten Rock, in the wilderness, the work of the Trinity illustrated.

> "Behold, I will stand before thee there upon the rock in Horeb; and thou shall smite the rock, and there shall come water out of it, that the people may drink. And Moses did so, in the sight of the elders of Israel."

Paul declares, in Corinthians, that the rock was Christ; it represented Christ. God says: "I will stand upon the rock," and as Moses smote the rock the water came out, which was an emblem of the Holy Spirit; and it flowed out along through the camp; and they drank of the water. Now water is cleansing; it is fertilizing; it is refreshing; it is abundant, and it is freely given; and so the Spirit of God is the same: cleansing, fertilizing, refreshing, reviving, and He was freely given when the smitten Christ was glorified. Then, too, fire is an emblem of the Spirit; it is purifying, illuminating, searching. We talk about searching our hearts. We can not do it. What we want is to have God search them. O that God may search us and bring out the hidden things, the secret things that cluster there and bring them to light.

The wind is another emblem. It is independent, powerful, sensible in its effects, and reviving; how the Spirit of God revives when He comes to all the drooping members of the Church. Then the rain and the dew — fertilizing, refreshing, abundant; and the dove, gentle — what more gentle than the dove; and the lamb? — gentle, meek, innocent, a sacrifice. We read of the wrath of God; we read of the wrath of the Lamb, but nowhere do we read of the wrath of the Holy Spirit — gentle, innocent, meek, loving; and that Spirit wants to take possession of our hearts. And He comes as a voice, another emblem — speaking, guiding, warning, teaching; and the seal — impressing, securing, and making us as His own. May we know Him in all His wealth of blessing. This is my prayer for myself — for you.

May we heed the words of the grand Apostle:

> "My speech and my preaching was not with enticing words of man's wisdom, but in demonstration of the Spirit, and of power: that your faith should not stand in the wisdom of men, but in the power of God."

THE OVERCOMING LIFE
AND OTHER SERMONS

By
D. L. MOODY.

"*This is the victory that overcometh the, world, even our faith.*"
COPYRIGHTED 1896.

Chapter 1

THE CHRISTIAN'S WARFARE

I would like to have you open your Bible at the first epistle of John, fifth chapter, fourth and fifth verses: "Whatsoever is born of God overcometh the world: and this is the victory that overcometh the world, even our faith. Who is he that overcometh the world, but he that believeth that Jesus is the Son of God?"

When a battle is fought, all are anxious to know who are the victors. In these verses we are told who is to gain the victory in life. When I was converted I made this mistake: I thought the battle was already mine, the victory already won, the crown already in my grasp. I thought that old things had passed away, that all things had become new; that my old corrupt nature, the Adam life, was gone. But I found out, after serving Christ for a few months, that conversion was only like enlisting in the army, that there was a battle on hand, and that if I was to get a crown, I had to work for it and fight for it.

Salvation is a gift, as free as the air we breathe. It is to be obtained, like any other gift, without money and without price: there are no other terms. "To him that worketh not, but believeth." But on the other hand, if we are to gain a crown, we must work for it. Let me quote a few verses in First Corinthians:

> "For other foundation can no man lay than that which is laid, which is Jesus Christ. But if any man buildeth on the foundation gold, silver, costly stones, wood, hay, stubble; each man's work shall be made manifest: for the day shall declare it, because it is revealed in fire: and the fire itself shall prove each man's work, of what sort it is. If any man's work shall abide, which he built thereon, he shall receive a reward. If any man's work shall be burned, he shall suffer loss: but he himself shall be saved; yet so as through fire."

We see clearly from this that we may be saved, but all our works burned up. I may have a wretched, miserable voyage through life, with no victory, and no reward at the end; saved, yet so as by fire, or as Job puts it, "with the skin of my teeth." I believe that a great many men will barely get to heaven as Lot got out of Sodom, burned out, nothing left, works and everything else destroyed.

It is like this: when a man enters the army, he is a member of the army the moment he enlists; he is just as much a member as a man who has been in the army ten or twenty years. But enlisting is one thing, and participating in a battle another. Young converts are like those just enlisted.

It is folly for any man to attempt to fight in his own strength. The world, the flesh and the devil are too much for any man. But if we are linked to Christ by faith, and He is formed in us the hope of glory, then we shall get the victory over every enemy. It is believers who are the overcomers. "Thanks be unto God, which always causeth us to triumph in Christ." Through Him we shall be more than conquerors.

I wouldn't think of talking to unconverted men about overcoming the world, for it is utterly impossible. They might as well try to cut down the American forest with their penknives. But a good many Christian people make this mistake: they think the battle is already fought and won. They have an idea that all they have to do is to put the oars down in the bottom of the boat, and the current will drift them into the ocean of God's eternal love. But we have to cross the current. We have to learn how to watch and fight, and how to overcome. The battle is only just commenced. The Christian life is a conflict and a warfare, and the quicker we find it out the better. There is not a blessing in this world that God has not linked Himself to. All the great and higher blessings God associates with Himself. When God and man work together, then it is that there is going to be victory. We are coworkers with Him. You might take a mill, and put it forty feet above a river, and there isn't capital enough in the States to make that river turn the mill; but get it down about forty feet, and away it works. We want to keep in mind that if we are going to overcome the world, we have got to work with God. It is His power that makes all the means of grace effectual.

The story is told that Frederick Douglas, the great slave orator, once said in a mournful speech when things looked dark for his race: —

> "The white man is against us, governments are against us, the spirit of the times is against us. I see no hope for the colored race. I am full of sadness."

Just then a poor old colored woman rose in the audience, and said. —

"Frederick, is God dead?"

My friend, it makes a difference when you count God in.

Now many a young believer is discouraged and disheartened when he realizes this warfare. He begins to think that God has forsaken him, that Christianity is not all that it professes to be. But he should rather regard it as an encouraging sign. No sooner has a soul escaped from his snare than the great Adversary takes steps to ensnare it again. He puts forth all his power to recapture his lost prey. The fiercest attacks are made on the strongest forts, and the fiercer the battle the young believer is called on to wage, the surer evidence it is of the work of the Holy Spirit in his heart. God will not desert him in his time of need, any more than He deserted His people of old when they were hard pressed by their foes.

The Only Complete Victor

This brings me to the fourth verse of the fourth chapter of the same epistle: "Ye are of God, little children, and have overcome them: because greater is He that is in you than he that is in the world." The only man that ever conquered this world — was complete victor — was Jesus Christ. When He shouted on the cross, "It is finished!" it was the shout of a conqueror. He had overcome every enemy. He had met sin and death. He had met every foe that you and I have got to meet, and had come off victor. Now if I have got the spirit of Christ, if I have got that same life in me, then it is that I have got a power that is greater than any power in the world, and with that same power I overcome the world.

Notice that everything human in this world fails. Every man, the moment he takes his eye off God, has failed. Every man has been a failure at some period of his life. Abraham failed. Moses failed. Elijah failed. Take the men that have become so famous and that were so mighty — the moment they got their eye off God, they were weak like other men; and it is a very singular thing that those men failed on the strongest point in their character. I suppose it was because they were not on the watch. Abraham was noted for his faith, and he failed right there — he denied his wife. Moses was noted for his meekness and humility, and he failed right there — he got angry. God kept him out of the promised land because he lost his temper. I know he was called "the servant of God," and that he was a mighty man, and had power with God, but humanly speaking, he failed, and was kept out of the promised land.

Elijah was noted for his power in prayer and for his courage, yet he became a coward. He was the boldest man of his day, and stood before Ahab, and the royal court, and all the prophets of Baal; yet when he heard that Jezebel had threatened his life, he ran away to the desert, and under a juniper tree prayed that he might die. Peter was noted for his boldness, and a little maid scared him nearly out of his wits. As soon as she spoke to him, he began to tremble, and he swore that he didn't know Christ. I have often said to myself that I'd like to have been there on the day of Pentecost alongside of that maid when she saw Peter preaching.

"Why," I suppose she said, "what has come over that man? He was afraid of me only a few weeks ago, and now he stands up before all Jerusalem and charges these very Jews with the murder of Jesus."

The moment he got his eye off the Master he failed; and every man, I don't care who he is — even the strongest — every man that hasn't Christ in him, is a failure. John, the beloved disciple, was noted for his meekness; and yet we hear of him wanting to call fire down from heaven on a little town because it had refused the common hospitalities.

Triumphs of Faith

Now, how are we to get the victory over all our enemies? Turn to Galatians, second chapter, verse twenty: "I am crucified with Christ; nevertheless I live; yet not I, but Christ liveth in me: and the life which I now live in the flesh, I live by the faith of the Son of God, who loved me and gave Himself for me." We live by faith. We get this life by faith, and become linked to Immanuel — "God with us." If I have God for me, I am going to overcome. How do we gain this mighty power? By faith.

The next passage I want to call your attention to is Romans, chapter eleven, verse twenty: "Because of unbelief they were broken off; and thou standest by faith." The Jews were cut off on account of their unbelief: we were grafted in on account of our belief. So notice: We live by faith, and we stand by faith.

Next: We walk by faith. Second Corinthians, chapter five, verse seven: "For we walk by faith, not by sight." The most faulty Christians I know are those who want to walk by sight. They want to see the end — how a thing is going to come out. That isn't walking by faith at all — that is walking by sight.

I think the characters that best represent this difference are Joseph and Jacob. Jacob was a man who walked with God by sight. You remember his vow at Bethel: — "If God will be with me, and will keep me in this way that I go, and will give me bread to eat, and raiment to put on, so that I come again to my father's house in peace; then shall the Lord be my God." And you remember how his heart revived when he saw the wagons Joseph sent him from Egypt. He sought after signs. He never could have gone through the temptations and trials that his son Joseph did. Joseph represents a higher type of Christian. He could walk in the dark. He could survive thirteen years of misfortune, in spite of his dreams, and then ascribe it all to the goodness and providence of God.

Lot and Abraham are a good illustration Lot turned away from Abraham and tented on the plains of Sodom. He got a good stretch of pasture land, but he had bad neighbors. He was a weak character and he should have kept with Abraham in order to get strong. A good many men are just like that. As long as their mothers are living, or they are bolstered up by some godly person, they get along very well; but they can't stand alone. Lot walked by sight; but Abraham walked by faith; he went out in the footsteps of God. "By faith Abraham, when he was called to go out into a place which he should after receive for an inheritance, obeyed; and he went out, not knowing whither he went. By faith he sojourned in the land of promise, as in a strange country, dwelling in tabernacles with Isaac and Jacob, the heirs with him of the same promise: for he looked for a city which hath foundations, whose builder and maker is God."

And again: We fight by faith. Ephesians, sixth chapter, verse sixteen: "Above all, taking the shield of faith, wherewith ye shall be able to quench all the fiery darts of the wicked." Every dart Satan can fire at us we can quench by faith, By faith we can overcome the Evil One. To fear is to have more faith in your antagonist than in Christ.

Some of the older people can remember when our war broke out. Secretary Seward, who was Lincoln's Secretary of State — a long-headed and shrewd politician — prophesied that the war would be over in ninety days; and young men in thousands and hundreds of thousands came forward and volunteered to go down to Dixie and whip the South. They thought they would be back in ninety days; but the war lasted four years, and cost about half a million of lives. What was the matter? Why, the South was a good deal stronger than the North supposed. Its strength was underestimated.

Jesus Christ makes no mistake of that kind. When He enlists a man in His service, He shows him the dark side; He lets him know that he must live a life of self-denial. If a man is not willing to go to heaven by the way of Calvary, he cannot go at all. Many men want a religion in which there is no cross, but they cannot enter heaven that way. If we are to be disciples of Jesus Christ, we must deny ourselves and take up our cross and follow Him. So let us sit down and count the cost. Do not think that you will have no battles if you follow the Nazarene, because many battles are before you. Yet if I had ten thousand lives, Jesus Christ should have every one of them. Men do not object to a battle if they are confident that they will have victory, and, thank God, every one of us may have the victory if we will.

The reason why so many Christians fail all through life is just this — they under-estimate the strength of the enemy. My dear friend; you and I have got a terrible enemy to contend with. Don't let Satan deceive you. Unless you are spiritually dead, it means warfare. Nearly everything around tends to draw us away from God. We do not step clear out of Egypt on to the throne of God. There is the wilderness journey, and there are enemies in the land.

Don't let any man or woman think all he or she has to do is to join the church. That will not save you. The question is, are you overcoming the world, or is the world overcoming you? Are you more patient than you were five years ago? Are you more amiable? If you are not, the world is overcoming you, even if you are a church member. That epistle that Paul wrote to Titus says that we are to be sound in patience, faith and charity. We have got Christians, a good many of them, that are good in spots, but mighty poor in other spots. Just a little bit of them seems to be saved, you know. They are not rounded out in their characters. It is just because they haven't been taught that they have a terrible foe to overcome.

If I wanted to find out whether a Man was a Christian, I wouldn't go to his minister. I would go and ask his wife. I tell you, we want more home piety just now. If a man doesn't treat his wife right, I don't want to hear him talk about Christianity. What is the use of his talking about salvation for the next life, if he has no salvation for this? We want a Christianity that goes into our homes and everyday lives. Some men's religion just repels me. They put on a whining voice and a sort of a religious tone, and talk so sanctimoniously on Sunday that you would think they were wonderful saints. But on Monday they are quite different. They put their religion away with their clothes, and you don't see any more of it until the next Sunday. You laugh, but let us look out that we don't belong to that class. My friend, we have got to have a higher type of Christianity, or the Church is gone. It is wrong for a man or woman to profess what they don't possess. If you are not overcoming temptations, the world is overcoming you. Just get on your knees and ask God to help you. My dear friends, let us go to God and ask Him to search us. Let us ask Him to wake us up, and let us not think that just because we are church members we are all right. We are all wrong if we are not getting victory over sin.

Chapter 2

INTERNAL FOES.

Now if we are going to overcome, we must begin inside. God always begins there. An enemy inside the fort is far more dangerous than one outside.

Scripture teaches that in every believer there are two natures warring against each other. Paul says in his epistle to the Romans: — "For we know that the law is spiritual: but I am carnal, sold under sin. For that which I do I allow not: for what I would, that do I not; but what I hate, that do I. If then I do that which I would not, I consent unto the law that it is good. Now then it is no more I that do it, but sin that dwelleth in me. For I know that in me (that is, in my flesh) dwelleth no good thing: for to will is present with me; but how to perform that which is good I find not. For the good that I would I do not: but the evil which I would not, that I do. Now if I do that I would not, it is no more I that do it, but sin that dwelleth in me. I find then a law, that when I would do good, evil is present with me. For I delight in the law of God after the inward man: but I see another law in my members, warring against the law of my mind, and bringing me into captivity to the law of sin which is in my members."

Again, in the Epistle to the Galatians, he says: "For the flesh lusteth against the Spirit, and the Spirit against the flesh: and these are contrary the one to the other: so that ye cannot do the things that ye would."

When we are born of God, we get His nature, but He does not immediately take away all the old nature. Each species of animal and bird is true to its nature. You can tell the nature of the dove or canary bird. The horse is true to his nature, the cow is true to hers. But a man has two natures, and do not let the world or Satan make you think that the old nature is extinct, because it is not. "Reckon ye yourselves dead"; but if you were dead, you wouldn't need to reckon yourselves dead, would you? The dead self would be dropped out of the reckoning. "I keep my body under"; if it were dead, Paul wouldn't have needed to keep it under. I am judicially dead, but the old nature is alive, and therefore if I don't keep my body under and crucify the flesh with its affections, this lower nature will gain the advantage, and I shall be in bondage.

Many men live all their lives in bondage to the old nature, when they might have liberty if they would only live this overcoming life. The old Adam never dies. It remains corrupt. "From the sole of the foot even unto the head there is no soundness in it; but wounds, and bruises, and putrifying sores: they have not been closed, neither bound up, neither mollified with ointment."

A gentleman in India once got a tiger-cub, and tamed it so that it became a pet. One day when it had grown up, it tasted blood, and the old tiger-nature flashed out, and it had to be killed. So with the old nature in the believer. It never dies, though it is subdued: and unless he is watchful and prayerful, it will gain the upper hand, and rush him into sin. Someone has pointed out that "I" is the centre of S-I-N. It is the medium through which Satan acts.

And so the worst enemy you have to overcome, after all, is yourself. When Capt. T— became converted in London, he was a great society man. After he had been a Christian some months, he was asked;

"What have you found to be your greatest enemy since you began to be a Christian?"

After a few minutes of deep thought he said, "Well, I think it is myself."

"Ah!" said the lady, "the King has taken you into His presence, for it is only in His presence that we are taught these truths."

I have had more trouble with D. L. Moody than with any other man who has crossed my path. If I can only keep him right, I don't have any trouble with other people. A good many have trouble with servants. Did you ever think that the trouble lies with you instead of the servants? If one member of the family is constantly snapping, he will have the whole family snapping. It is true whether you believe it or not. You speak quickly and snappishly to people and they will do the same to you.

Appetite

Now take appetite. That is an enemy inside. How many young men are ruined by the appetite for strong drink! Many a young man has grown up to be a curse to his father and mother, instead of a blessing. Not long ago the body of a young suicide was discovered in one of our large cities. In his pocket was found a paper on which he had written: "I have done this myself. Don't tell anyone. It is all through drink." An intimation of these facts in the public press drew two hundred and forty six letters from two hundred and forty six families, each of whom had a prodigal son who, it was feared, might be the suicide.

Strong drink is an enemy, both to body and soul. It is reported that Sir Andrew Clarke, the celebrated London physician, once made the following statement: "Now let me say that I am speaking solemnly and carefully when I tell you that I am considerably within the mark in saying that within the rounds of my hospital wards today, seven out of every ten that lie there in their beds owe their ill health to alcohol. I do not say that seventy in every hundred are drunkards; I do not know that one of them is; but they use alcohol. So soon as a man begins to take one drop, then the desire begotten in him becomes a part of his nature, and that nature, formed by his acts, inflicts curses inexpressible when handed down to the generations that are to follow him as part and parcel of their being. When I think of this I am disposed to give up my profession — to give up everything — and to go forth upon a holy crusade to preach to all men, 'Beware of this enemy of the race!'"

It is the most destructive agency in the world today. It kills more than the bloodiest wars. It is the fruitful parent of crime and idleness and poverty and disease. It spoils a man for this world, and damns him for the next. The Word of God has declared it: "Be not deceived: neither fornicators, nor idolaters, nor adulterers, . . . nor drunkards . . . shall inherit the Kingdom of God."

How can we overcome this enemy? Bitter experience proves that man is not powerful enough in his own strength. The only cure for the accursed appetite is regeneration — a new life — the power of the risen Christ within us. Let a man that is given to strong drink look to God for help, and He will give him victory over his appetite. Jesus Christ came to destroy the works of the devil, and He will take away that appetite if you will let Him.

Temper

Then there is temper. I wouldn't give much for a man that hasn't temper. Steel isn't good for anything if it hasn't got temper. But when temper gets the mastery over me I am its slave, and it is a source of weakness. It may be made a great power for good all through my life, and help me; or it may become my greatest enemy from within, and rob me of power. The current in some rivers is so strong as to make them useless for navigation.

Someone has said that a preacher will never miss the people when he speaks of temper. It is astonishing how little mastery even professing Christians have over it. A friend of mine in England was out visiting, and while sitting in the parlor, heard an awful noise in the hall. He asked what it meant, and was told that it was only the doctor throwing his boots downstairs because they were not properly blacked. "Many Christians," said an old divine, "who bore the loss of a child or of all their property with the most heroic Christian fortitude, are entirely vanquished by the breaking of a dish or the blunders of a servant."

I have had people say to me, "Mr. Moody, how can I get control of my temper?"

If you really want to get control, I will tell you how, but you won't like the medicine. Treat it as a sin and confess it. People look upon it as a sort of a misfortune, and one lady told me she inherited it from her father and mother. Supposing she did. That is no excuse for her.

When you get angry again and speak unkindly to a person, and when you realize it, go and ask that person to forgive you. You won't get mad with that person for the next twenty-four hours. You might do it in about forty eight hours, but go the second time, and after you have done it about half-a-dozen times, you will get out of the business, because it makes the old flesh burn.

A lady said to me once, "I have got so in the habit of exaggerating that my friends accuse me of exaggerating so that they don't understand me."

She said, "Can you help me? What can I do to overcome it?"

"Well," I said, "the next time you catch yourself lying, go right to that party and say you have lied, and tell him you are sorry. Say it is a lie; stamp it out, root and branch; that is what you want to do."

"Oh," she said, "I wouldn't like to call it lying." But that is what it was.

Christianity isn't worth a snap of your finger if it doesn't straighten out your character. I have got tired of all mere gush and sentiment. If people can't tell when you are telling the truth, there is something radically wrong, and you had better straighten it out right away. Now, are you ready to do it? Bring yourself to it whether you want to or not. Do you find someone who has been offended by something you have done? Go right to them and tell them you are sorry. You say you are not to blame. Never mind, go right to them, and tell them you are sorry. I have had to do it a good many times. An impulsive man like myself has to do it often, but I sleep all the sweeter at night when I get things straightened out. Confession never fails to bring a blessing. I have sometimes had to get off the platform and go down and ask a man's forgiveness before I could go on preaching.

A Christian man ought to be a gentleman every time; but if he is not, and he finds he has wounded or hurt someone, he ought to go and straighten it out at once. You know there are a great many people who want just Christianity enough to make them respectable. They don't think about this overcoming life that gets the victory all the time. They have their blue days and their cross days, and the children say,

"Mother is cross today, and you will have to be very careful."

We don't want any of these touchy blue days; these ups and downs. If we are overcoming, that is the effect our life is going to have on others, they will have confidence in our Christianity. The reason that many a man has no power, is that there is some cursed sin covered up. There will not be a drop of dew until that sin is brought to light. Get right inside. Then we can go out like giants and conquer the world if everything is right within.

Paul says that we are to be sound in faith, in patience, and in love. If a man is unsound in his faith, the clergy take the ecclesiastical sword and cut him off at once. But he may be ever so unsound in charity, in patience, and nothing is said about that. We must be sound in faith, in love, and in patience if we are to be true to God.

How delightful it is to meet a man who can control his temper! It is said of Wilberforce that a friend once found him in the greatest agitation, looking for a dispatch he had mislaid, for which one of the royal family was waiting. Just then, as if to make it still more trying, a disturbance was heard in the nursery.

"Now," thought the friend, "surely his temper will give way."

The thought had hardly passed through his mind when Wilberforce turned to him and said:

> "What a blessing it is to hear those dear children! Only think what a relief, among other hurries, to hear their voices and know they are well."

Covetousness

Take the sin of covetousness. There is more said in the Bible against it than against drunkenness. I must get it out of me — destroy it, root and branch — and not let it have dominion over me. We think that a man who gets drunk is a horrid monster, but a covetous man will often be received into the church, and put into office, who is as vile and black in the sight of God as any drunkard.

The most dangerous thing about this sin is that it is not generally regarded as very heinous. Of course we all have a contempt for misers, but all covetous men are not misers. Another thing to be noted about it is that it fastens upon the old rather than upon the young.

Let us see what the Bible says about covetousness: —

"Mortify therefore your members . . . covetousness, which is idolatry."

"No covetous man hath any inheritance in the Kingdom of God."

"They that will be (that is, desire to be) rich fall into temptation and a snare, and into many foolish and hurtful lusts, which drown men in destruction and perdition. For the love of money is the root of all evil: which while some coveted after, they have erred from the faith, and pierced themselves through with many sorrows."

"The wicked blesseth the covetous, whom the Lord abhorreth."

Covetousness enticed Lot into Sodom. It caused the destruction of Achan and all his house. It was the iniquity of Balaam. It was the sin of Samuel's sons. It left Gehazi a leper. It sent the rich young ruler away sorrowful. It led Judas to sell his Master and Lord. It brought about the death of Ananias and Sapphira. It was the blot in the character of Felix. What victims it has had in all ages!

Do you say: "How am I going to check covetousness?"

Well, — I don't think there is any difficulty about that. If you find yourself getting very covetous — very miserly — wanting to get everything you can into your possession — just begin to scatter. Just say to covetousness that you will strangle it, and rid it out of your disposition.

A wealthy farmer in New York state, who had been a noted miser, a very selfish man, was converted. Soon after his conversion a poor man came to him one day to ask for help. He had been burned out, and had no provisions. This young convert thought he would be liberal and give him a ham from his smoke house. He started toward the smoke-house, and on the way the tempter said,

"Give him the smallest one you have."

He struggled all the way as to whether he would give a large or a small one. In order to overcome his selfishness, he took down the biggest ham and gave it to the man.

The tempter said, "You are a fool."

But he replied, "If you don't keep still, I will give him every ham I have in the smoke-house."

If you find that you are selfish, give something. Determine to overcome that spirit of selfishness, and to keep your body under, no matter what it may cost.

Mr. Durant told me he was engaged by Goodyear to defend the rubber patent, and he was to have half of the money that came from the patent, if he succeeded. One day he woke up to find that he was a rich man, and he said that the greatest struggle of his life then took place as to whether he would let money be his master, or he be master of money, whether he would be its slave, or make it a slave to him. At last he got the victory, and that is how Wellesley College was built.

Are You Jealous, Envious?

Go and do a good turn for that person of whom you are jealous. That is the way to cure jealousy; it will kill it. Jealousy is a devil, it is a horrid monster. The poets imagined that Envy dwelt in a dark cave, being pale and thin, looking asquint, never rejoicing except in the misfortune of others, and hurting himself continually.

There is a fable of an eagle which could out fly another, and the other didn't like it. The latter saw a sportsman one day, and said to him,

"I wish you would bring down that eagle."

The sportsman replied that he would if he only had some feathers to put into the arrow. So the eagle pulled one out of his wing. The arrow was shot, but didn't quite reach the rival eagle; it was flying too high. The envious eagle pulled out more feathers, and kept pulling them out until he lost so many that he couldn't fly, and then the sportsman turned around and killed him. My friend, if you are jealous, the only man you can hurt is yourself.

There were two business men — merchants — and there was great rivalry between them, a great deal of bitter feeling. One of them was converted. He went to his minister and said,

"I am still jealous of that man, and I do not know how to overcome it."

"Well," he said, "if a man comes into your store to buy goods, and you cannot supply him, just send him over to your neighbor."

He said he wouldn't like to do that.

"Well," the minister said, "you do it and you will kill jealousy."

He said he would, and when a customer came into his store for goods which he did not have, he would tell him to go across the street to his neighbor's. By and by the other began to send his customers over to this man's store, and the breach was healed.

Pride

Then there is pride. This is another of those sins which the Bible so strongly condemns, but which the world hardly reckons as a sin at all. "An high look and a proud heart is sin." "Everyone that is proud in heart is an abomination to the Lord; though hand join in hand, he shall not be unpunished." Christ included pride among those evil things which, proceeding out of the heart of a man, defile him.

People have an idea that it is just the wealthy who are proud. But go down on some of the back streets, and you will find that some of the very poorest are as proud as the richest. It is the heart, you know. People that haven't any money are just as proud as those that have. We have got to crush it out. It is an enemy. You needn't be proud of your face, for there is not one but that after ten days in the grave the worms would be eating your body. There is nothing to be proud of — is there? Let us ask God to deliver us from pride.

You can't fold your arms and say, "Lord, take it out of me"; but just go and work with Him.

Mortify your pride by cultivating humility. "Put on, therefore," says Paul, "as the elect of God, holy and beloved, . . . humbleness of mind." "Be clothed with humility," says Peter. "Blessed are the poor in spirit."

Chapter 3

EXTERNAL FOES

What are our enemies without? What does James say? "Know ye not that the friendship of the world is enmity with God? whosoever therefore will be a friend of the world is the enemy of God." And John? "Love not the world, neither the things that are in the world. If any man love the world, the love of the Father is not in him."

Now, people want to know what is the world. When you talk with them they say:

"Well, when you say 'the world,' what do you mean?"

Here we have the answer in the next verse: "For all that is in the world, the lust of the flesh, and the lust of the eyes, and the pride of life, is not of the Father, but is of the world. And the world passeth away, and the lust thereof: but he that doeth the will of God abideth forever."

"The world" does not mean nature around us. God nowhere tells us that the material world is an enemy to be overcome. On the contrary, we read: "The earth is the Lord's, and the fullness thereof; the world, and they that dwell therein." "The heavens declare the glory of God; and the firmament sheweth His handywork."

It means "human life and society as far as alienated from God, through being centered on material aims and objects, and thus opposed to God's Spirit and kingdom." Christ said: "If the world hate you, ye know that it hated Me before it hated you . . . the world hath hated them because they are not of the world, even as I am not of the world." Love of the world means the forgetfulness of the eternal future by reason of love for passing things.

How can the world be overcome? Not by education, not by experience; only by faith. "This is the victory that overcometh the world, even our faith. Who is he that overcometh the world, but he that believeth that Jesus is the Son of God?"

Worldly Habits and Fashions

For one thing we must fight worldly habits and fashions. We must often go against the customs of the world. I have great respect for a man who can stand up for what he believes is right against all the world. He who can stand alone is a hero.

Suppose it is the custom for young men to do certain things you wouldn't like your mother to know of — things that your mother taught you are wrong. You may have to stand up alone among all your companions.

They will say: "You can't get away from your mother, eh? Tied to your mother's apron strings!"

But just you say: "Yes! I have some respect for my mother. She taught me what is right, and she is the best friend I have. I believe that is wrong, and I am going to stand for the right." If you have to stand alone, stand. Enoch did it, and Joseph, and Elisha, and Paul. God has kept such men in all ages.

Someone says: "I move in society where they have wine parties. I know it is rather a dangerous thing because my son is apt to follow me. But I can stop just where I want to; perhaps my son hasn't got the same power as I have, and he may go over the dam. But it is the custom in the society where I move."

Once I got into a place where I had to get up and leave. I was invited into a home, and they had a late supper, and there were seven kinds of liquor on the table. I am ashamed to say they were Christian people. A deacon urged a young lady to drink until her face flushed. I rose from the table and went out; I felt that it was no place for me. They considered me very rude. That was going against custom; that was entering a protest against such an infernal thing. Let us go against custom, when it leads astray.

I was told in a southern college, some years ago, that no man was considered a first class gentleman who did not drink. Of course it is not so now.

Pleasure

Another enemy is worldly pleasure. A great many people are just drowned in pleasure. They have no time for any meditation at all. Many a man has been lost to society, and lost to his family, by giving himself up to the god of pleasure. God wants His children to be happy, but in a way that will help and not hinder them.

A lady came to me once and said: "Mr. Moody, I wish you would tell me how I can become a Christian." The tears were rolling down her cheeks, and she was in a very favorable mood; "but," she said, "I don't want to be one of your kind."

"Well," I asked, "have I got any peculiar kind? What is the matter with my Christianity?"

"Well," she said, "my father was a doctor, and had a large practice, and he used to get so tired that he used to take us to the theater. There was a large family of girls, and we had tickets for the theaters three or four times a week. I suppose we were there a good deal oftener than we were in church. I am married to a lawyer, and he has a large practice. He gets so tired that he takes us out to the theater," and she said, "I am far better acquainted with the theater and theater people than with the church and church people, and I don't want to give up the theater."

"Well," I said, "did you ever hear me say anything about theaters? There have been reporters here every day for all the different papers, and they are giving my sermons verbatim in one paper. Have you ever seen anything in the sermons against the theaters?"

She said, "No."

"Well," I said, "I have seen you in the audience every afternoon for several weeks and have you heard me say anything against theaters?"

No, she hadn't.

"Well," I said, "what made you bring them up?" "Why, I supposed you didn't believe in theaters." "What made you think that?"

"Why," she said, "Do you ever go?"

"No."

"Why don't you go?"

"Because I have got something better. I would sooner go out into the street and eat dirt than do some of the things I used to do before I became a Christian."

"Why!" she said, "I don't understand."

"Never mind," I said. "When Jesus Christ has the pre-eminence, you will understand it all. He didn't come down here and say we shouldn't go here and we shouldn't go there, and lay down a lot of rules; but He laid down great principles. Now, He says if you love Him you will take delight in pleasing Him." And I began to preach Christ to her. The tears started again. She said:

"I tell you, Mr. Moody, that sermon on the indwelling Christ yesterday afternoon just broke my heart. I admire Him, and I want to be a Christian, but I don't want to give up the theaters."

I said, "Please don't mention them again. I don't want to talk about theaters. I want to talk to you about Christ." So I took my Bible, and I read to her about Christ.

But she said again, "Mr. Moody, can I go to the theater if I become a Christian?"

"Yes," I said, "you can go to the theater just as much as you like if you are a real, true Christian, and can go with His blessing."

"Well," she said, "I am glad you are not so narrow-minded as some."

She felt quite relieved to think that she could go to the theaters and be a Christian. But I said,

"If you can go to the theater for the glory of God, keep on going; only be sure that you go for the glory of God. If you are a Christian you will be glad to do whatever will please Him."

I really think she became a Christian that day. The burden had gone, there was joy; but just as she was leaving me at the door, she said,

"I am not going to give up the theater."

In a few days she came back to me and said, "Mr. Moody, I understand all about that theater business now. I went the other night. There was a large party at our house, and my husband wanted us to go, and we went; but when the curtain lifted, everything looked so different. I said to my husband, 'This is no place for me;

this is horrible. I am not going to stay here, I am going home.' He said, 'Don't make a fool of yourself. Everyone has heard that you have been converted in the Moody meetings, and if you go out, it will be all through fashionable society, I beg of you don't make a fool of yourself by getting up and going out.' But I said, 'I have been making a fool of myself all of my life.'"

Now, the theater hadn't changed, but she had got something better and she was going to overcome the world. "They that are after the flesh do mind the things of the flesh; but they that are after the Spirit the things of the Spirit." When Christ has the first place in your heart you are going to get victory. Just do whatever you know will please Him. The great objection I have to these things is that they get the mastery, and become a hindrance to spiritual growth.

Business

It may be that we have got to overcome in business. Perhaps it is business morning, noon and night, and Sundays, too. When a man will drive like Jehu all the week and like a snail on Sunday, isn't there something wrong with him? Now, business is legitimate; and a man is not, I think, a good citizen that will not go out and earn his bread by the sweat of his brow; and he ought to be a good business man, and whatever he does, do thoroughly. At the same time, if he lays his whole heart on his business, and makes a god of it, and thinks more of it than anything else, then the world has come in. It may be very legitimate in its place — like fire, which, in its place, is one of the best friends of man; out of place, is one of the worst enemies of man; — like water, which we cannot live without; and yet, when not in place, it becomes an enemy.

So my friends, that is the question for you and me to settle. Now look at yourself. Are you getting the victory? Are you growing more even in your disposition? are you getting mastery over the world and the flesh?

And bear this in mind: Every temptation you overcome makes you stronger to overcome others, while every temptation that defeats you makes you weaker. You can become weaker and weaker, or you can become stronger and stronger. Sin takes the pith out of your sinews, but virtue makes you stronger. How many men have been overcome by some little thing! Turn a moment to the Song of Solomon, the second chapter, fifteenth verse: "Take us the foxes, the little foxes that spoil the vines: for our vines have tender grapes." A great many people seem to think these little things — getting out of patience, using little deceits, telling white lies (as they call them), and when somebody calls on you sending word by the servant you are not at home — all these are little things. Sometimes you can brace yourself up against a great temptation; and almost before you know it you fall before some little thing. A great many men are overcome by a little persecution.

Persecution

Do you know, I don't think we have enough persecution now-a-days. Some people say we have persecution that is just as hard to bear as in the Dark Ages. Anyway, I think it would be a good thing if we had a little of the old fashioned kind just now. It would bring out the strongest characters, and make us all healthier. I have heard men get up in prayer-meeting, and say they were going to make a few remarks, and then keep on till you would think they were going to talk all week. If we had a little persecution, people of that kind wouldn't talk so much. Spurgeon used to say some Christians would make good martyrs; they would burn well, they are so dry. If there were a few stakes for burning Christians, I think it would take all the piety out of some men. I admit they haven't got much; but then if they are not willing to suffer a little persecution for Christ, they are not fit to be His disciples. We are told: "All that will live godly in Christ Jesus shall suffer persecution." Make up your mind to this: If the world has nothing to say against you, Jesus Christ will have nothing to say for you.

The most glorious triumphs of the Church have been won in times of persecution. The early church was persecuted for about three hundred years after the crucifixion, and they were years of growth and progress. But then, as Saint Augustine has said, the cross passed from the scene of public executions to the diadem of the Caesars, and the down-grade movement began. When the Church has joined hands with the State, it has invariably retrograded in spirituality and effectiveness; but the opposition of the State has only served to purify it of all dross. It was persecution that gave Scotland to Presbyterianism. It was persecution that gave this country to civil and religious freedom.

How are we to overcome in time of persecution? Hear the words of Christ: "In the world ye shall have tribulation: but be of good cheer: I have overcome the world." Paul could testify that though persecuted, he was never forsaken; that the Lord stood by him, and strengthened him, and delivered him out of all his persecutions and afflictions.

A great many shrink from the Christian life because they will be sneered at. And then, sometimes when persecution won't bring a man down, flattery will. Foolish persons often come up to a man after he has preached and flatter him. Sometimes ladies do that. Perhaps they will say to some worker in the church: "You talk a great deal better than so-and-so"; and he becomes proud, and begins to strut around as if he was the most important person in the town. I tell you, we have a wily devil to contend with. If he can't overcome you with opposition, he will try flattery or ambition; and if that doesn't serve his purpose, perhaps there will come some affliction or disappointment, and he will overcome in way. But remember that anyone that has got Christ to help him can overcome every foe, and overcome them singly or collectively. Let them come. If we have got Christ within us, we will overthrow them all. Remember what Christ is able to do. In all the ages men have stood in greater temptations than you and I will ever have to meet.

Now, there is one more thing on this line: I have either got to overcome the world, or the world is going to overcome me. I have either got to conquer sin in me — or sin about me — and get it under my feet, or it is going to conquer me. A good many people are satisfied with one or two victories, and think that is all. I tell you, my dear friends, we have got to do something more than that. It is a battle all the time. We have this to encourage us: we are assured of victory at the end. We are promised a glorious triumph.

Eight "Overcomes"

Let me give you the eight "overcomes" of Revelation.
The first is:

"To him that overcometh will I give to eat of the tree of life." He shall have a right to the tree of life. When Adam fell, he lost that right. God turned him out of Eden lest he should eat of the tree of life and live as he was forever. Perhaps He just took that tree and transplanted it to the Garden above; and through the second Adam we are to have the right to eat of it.

Second:

"He that overcometh shall not be hurt of the second death." Death has no terrors for him, it cannot touch him. Why? Because Christ tasted death for every man. Hence he is on resurrection ground. Death may take this body, but that is all. This is only the house I live in. We need have no fear of death if we overcome.

Third:

"To him that overcometh will I give to eat of the hidden manna, and will give him a white stone, and in the stone a new name written, which no man knoweth saving he that receiveth it." If I overcome God will feed me with bread that the world knows nothing about, and give me a new name.

Fourth:

"He that overcometh, and keepeth My works unto the end, to him will I give power over the nations." Think of it! What a thing to have; power over the nations! A man that is able to rule himself is the man that God can trust with power. Only a man who can govern himself is fit to govern other men. I have an idea that we are down here in training, that God is just polishing us for some higher service. I don't know where the kingdoms are, but it we are to be kings and priests we must have kingdoms to reign over.

Fifth:

"He that overcometh, the same shall be clothed in white raiment; and I will not blot out his name out of the book of life, but I will confess his name before My Father, and before His angels." He shall present us to the Father in white garments, without spot or wrinkle. Every fault and stain shall be taken out, and we be made perfect. He that overcomes will not be a stranger in heaven.

Sixth:

"Him that overcometh will I make a pillar in the temple of My God; and he shall go no more out; and I will write upon him the name of My God and the name of the city of My God, which is New Jerusalem, which cometh down out of heaven from My God: and I write upon him My new name." Think of it! No more backsliding, no more wanderings over the dark mountains of sin, but forever with the King, and He says, "I will write upon him the name of My God." He is going to put His name upon us. Isn't it grand? Isn't it worth fighting for? It is said when Mahomet came in sight of Damascus and found that they had all left the city, he said: "If they won't fight for this city what will they fight for?" If men won't fight here for all this reward, what will they fight for?

Seventh:

"To him that overcometh will I grant to sit with Me in My throne, even as I also overcame, and am set down with My Father in His throne." My heart has often melted as I have looked at that. The Lord of Glory coming down and saying: "I will grant to you to sit on My throne, even as I sit on My Father's throne, if you will just overcome." Isn't it worth a struggle? How many will fight for a crown that is going to fade away! Yet we are to be placed above the angels, above the archangels, above the seraphim, above the cherubim, away up, upon the throne with Himself, and there we shall be forever with Him. May God put strength into every one of us to fight the battle of life, so that we may sit with Him on His throne. When Frederick of Germany was dying, his own son would not have been allowed to sit with him on the throne, nor to have let anyone else sit there with him. Yet we are told that we are joint heirs with Jesus Christ, and that we are to sit with Him in glory!

And now, the last I like best of all: "He that overcometh shall inherit all things; and I will be his God, and he shall be My son." My dear friends, isn't that a high calling? I used to have my Sabbath-school children sing — "I want to be an angel": but I have not done so for years. We shall be above angels: we shall be sons of God. Just see what a kingdom we shall come into: we shall inherit all things! Do you ask me how much I am worth? I don't know. The Rothschilds cannot compute their wealth. They don't know how many millions they own. That is my condition — I haven't the slightest idea how much I am worth. God has no poor children. If we overcome we shall inherit all things.

Oh, my dear friends, what an inheritance! Let us then get the victory, through Jesus Christ our Lord and Master.

Chapter 4

RESULTS OF TRUE REPENTANCE

I want to call your attention to what true repentance leads to. I am not addressing the unconverted only, because I am one of those who believe that there is a good deal of repentance to be done by the Church before much good will be accomplished in the world. I firmly believe that the low standard of Christian living is keeping a good many in the world and in their sins. When the ungodly see that Christian people do not repent, you cannot expect them to repent and turn away from their sins. I have repented ten thousand times more since I knew Christ than ever before; and I think most Christians have some things to repent of.

So now I want to preach to Christians as well as to the unconverted; to myself as well as to one who has never accepted Christ as his Savior.

There are five things that flow out of true repentance:

1. Conviction.
2. Contrition.
3. Confession of sin.
4. Conversion.
5. Confession of Jesus Christ before the world.

1. Conviction

When a man is not deeply convicted of sin, it is a pretty sure sign that he has not truly repented. Experience has taught me that men who have very slight conviction of sin, sooner or later lapse back into their old life. For the last few years I have been a good deal more anxious for a deep and true work in professing converts than I have for great numbers. If a man professes to be converted without realizing the heinousness of his sins, he is likely to be one of those stony ground hearers who don't amount to anything. The first breath of opposition, the first wave of persecution or ridicule, will suck them back into the world again.

I believe we are making a woeful mistake in taking so many people into the Church who have never been truly convicted of sin. Sin is just as black in a man's heart today as it ever was. I sometimes think it is blacker. For the more light a man has, the greater his responsibility, and therefore the greater need of deep conviction.

William Dawson once told this story to illustrate how humble the soul must be before it can find peace.

He said that at a revival meeting, a little lad who was used to Methodist ways, went home to his mother and said,

"Mother, John So-and-so is under conviction and seeking for peace, but he will not find it to-night, mother."

"Why, William?" said she.

"Because he is only down on one knee, mother, and he will never get peace until he is down on both knees."

Until conviction of sin brings us down on both knees, until we are completely humbled, until we have no hope in ourselves left, we cannot find the Savior.

There are three things that lead to conviction: (1) Conscience; (2) the Word of God; (3) the Holy Spirit. All three are used by God.

Long before we had any Word, God dealt with men through the conscience. That is what made Adam and Eve hide themselves from the presence of the Lord God among the trees of the Garden of Eden. That is what convicted Joseph's brethren when they said: "We are verily guilty concerning our brother in that we saw the anguish of his soul when he besought us and we would not hear. Therefore," said they (and remember, over twenty years had passed away since they had sold him into captivity), "therefore is this distress come upon us." That is what we must use with our children before they are old enough to understand about the Word and the Spirit of God. This is what accuses or excuses the heathen.

Conscience is "a divinely implanted faculty in man, telling him that he ought to do right." Someone has said that it was born when Adam and Eve ate of the forbidden fruit, when their eyes were opened and they "knew good and evil." It passes judgment, without being invited, upon our thoughts, words, and actions, approving or condemning according as it judges them to be right or wrong. A man cannot violate his conscience without being self-condemned.

But conscience is not a safe guide, because very often it will not tell you a thing is wrong until you have done it. It needs illuminating by God because it partakes of our fallen nature. Many a person does things that are wrong without being condemned by conscience. Paul said: "I verily thought with myself that I ought to do many things contrary to the name of Jesus of Nazareth." Conscience itself needs to be educated.

Again, conscience is too often like an alarm clock, which awakens and arouses at first, but after a time the man becomes used to it, and it loses its effect. Conscience can be smothered. I think we make a mistake in not preaching more to the conscience.

Hence, in due time, conscience was superseded by the law of God, which in time was fulfilled in Christ.

In this Christian land, where men have Bibles, these are the agency by which God produces conviction. The old Book tells you what is right and wrong before you commit sin, and what you need is to learn and appropriate its teachings, under the guidance of the Holy Spirit. Conscience compared with the Bible is as a candle compared with the sun in the heavens.

See how the truth convicted those Jews on the day of Pentecost. Peter, filled with the Holy Ghost, preached that "God hath made this same Jesus, whom ye have crucified, both Lord and Christ." "Now when they heard this, they were pricked in their heart, and said unto Peter and to the rest of the apostles, Men and brethren, what shall we do?"

Then, thirdly, the Holy Ghost convicts. I once heard the late Dr. A. J. Gordon expound that passage — "And when He (the

Comforter) is come, He will reprove the world of sin, of righteousness, and of judgment; of sin because they believe not on Me," — as follows: —

> "Some commentators say there was no real conviction of sin in the world until the Holy Ghost came. I think that foreign missionaries will say that that is not true, that a heathen who never heard of Christ may have a tremendous conviction of sin. For notice that God gave conscience first, and gave the Comforter afterward. Conscience bears witness to the law, the Comforter bears witness to Christ. Conscience brings legal conviction, the Comforter brings evangelical conviction. Conscience brings conviction unto condemnation, and the Comforter brings conviction unto justification. 'He shall convince the world of sin, because they believe not on Me.' That is the sin about which He convinces. It does not say that He convinces men of sin, because they have stolen or lied or committed adultery; but the Holy Ghost is to convince men of sin because they have not believed on Jesus Christ. The coming of Jesus Christ into the world made a sin possible that was not possible before. Light reveals darkness; it takes whiteness to bring conviction concerning blackness. There are negroes in Central Africa who never dreamed that they were black until they saw the face of a white man; and there are a great many people in this world that never knew they were sinful until they saw the face of Jesus Christ in all its purity.
>
> Jesus Christ now stands between us and the law. He has fulfilled the law for us. He has settled all claims of the law, and now whatever claim it had upon us has been transferred to Him, so that it is no longer the sin question, but the Son question, that confronts us. And, therefore, you notice that the first thing Peter does when he begins to preach after the Holy Ghost has been sent down is about Christ: 'Him being delivered by the determinate counsel of God, ye have taken and by wicked hands have crucified and slain.' It doesn't say a word about any other kind of sin. That is the sin that runs all through Peter's teaching, and as he preached, the Holy Ghost came down and convicted them, and they cried out, 'What shall we do to be saved?'
>
> Well, but we had no part in crucifying Christ; therefore, what is our sin? It is the same sin in another form. They were convicted of crucifying Christ; we are convicted because we have not believed on Christ crucified. They were convicted because they had despised and rejected God's Son. The Holy Ghost convicts us be-

cause we have not believed in the Despised and Rejected One. It is really the same sin in both cases — the sin of unbelief in Christ."

Some of the most powerful meetings I have ever been in were those in which there came a sort of hush over the people, and it seemed as if an unseen power gripped their consciences. I remember a man coming to one meeting, and the moment he entered, he felt that God was there. There came an awe upon him, and that very hour he was convicted and converted.

2. Contrition

The next thing is contrition, deep Godly sorrow and humiliation of heart because of sin. If there is not true contrition, a man will turn right back into the old sin. That is the trouble with many Christians.

A man may get angry, and if there is not much contrition, the next day he will get angry again. A daughter may say mean, cutting things to her mother, and then her conscience troubles her, and she says:
"Mother, I am sorry: forgive me."

But soon there is another outburst of temper, because the contrition is not deep and real. A husband speaks sharp words to his wife, and then to ease his conscience, he goes and buys her a bouquet of flowers. He will not go like a man and say he has done wrong.

What God wants is contrition, and if there is not contrition, there is not full repentance. "The Lord is nigh to the broken of heart, and saveth such as be contrite of spirit." "A broken and a contrite heart, O God, Thou wilt not despise." Many sinners are sorry for their sins, sorry that they cannot continue in sin; but they repent only with hearts that are not broken. I don't think we know how to repent now-a-days. We need some John the Baptist, wandering through the land, crying: "Repent! repent!"

3. Confession of Sin

If we have true contrition, that will lead us to confess our sins. I believe that nine-tenths of the trouble in our Christian life comes from failing to do this. We try to hide and cover up our sins; there is very little confession of them. Someone has said: "Unconfessed sin in the soul is like a bullet in the body."

If you have no power, it may be there is some sin that needs to be confessed, something in your life that needs straightening out. There is no amount of psalm-singing, no amount of attending religious meetings, no amount of praying or reading your Bible that is going to cover up anything of that kind. It must be confessed, and if I am too proud to confess, I need expect no mercy from God and no answers to my prayers. The Bible says: "He that covereth his sins shall not prosper." He may be a man in the pulpit, a priest behind the altar, a king on the throne; I don't care who he is. Man has been trying it for six thousand years. Adam tried it, and failed. Moses tried it when he buried the Egyptian whom he killed, but he failed. "Be sure your sin will find you out." You cannot bury your sin so deep but it will have a resurrection by and by, if it has not been blotted out by the Son of God. What man has failed to do for six thousand years, you and I had better give up trying to do.

There are three ways of confessing sin. All sin is against God, and must be confessed to Him. There are some sins I need never confess to anyone on earth. If the sin has been between myself and God, I may confess it alone in my closet: I need not whisper it in the ear of any mortal. "Father, I have sinned against heaven, and before Thee." "Against Thee, Thee only, have I sinned, and done this evil in Thy sight."

But if I have done some man a wrong, and he knows that I have wronged him, I must confess that sin not only to God but also to that man. If I have too much pride to confess it to him, I need not come to God. I may pray, and I may weep, but it will do no good. First confess to that man, and then go to God and see how quickly He will hear you, and send peace. "If thou bring thy gift to the altar, and there remember that thy brother hath aught against thee; leave there thy gift before the altar, and go thy ways. First be reconciled to thy brother, and then come and offer thy gift." That is the Scripture way.

Then there is another class of sins that must be confessed publicly. Suppose I have been known as a blasphemer, a drunkard, or a reprobate. If I repent of my sins, I owe the public a confession. The confession should be as public as the transgression. Many a person will say some mean thing about another in the presence of others, and then try to patch it up by going to that person alone. The confession should be made so that all who heard the transgression can hear it.

We are good at confessing other people's sins, but if it is true repentance, we shall have as much as we can do to look after our own. When a man or woman gets a good look into God's looking glass, he is not finding fault with other people: he has as much as he can do at home.

"If we confess our sins, He is faithful and just to forgive us our sins, and to cleanse us from all unrighteousness." Thank God for the Gospel! Church member, if there is any sin in your life, make up your mind that you will confess it, and be forgiven. Do not have any cloud between you and God. Be able to read your title clear to the mansion Christ has gone to prepare for you.

4. Conversion.

Confession leads to true conversion, and there is no conversion at all until these three steps have been taken.

Now the word "conversion" means two things. We say a man is "converted" when he is born again. But it also has a different meaning in the Bible. Peter said: "Repent, and be converted." The Revised Version reads: "Repent, and turn." Paul said that he was not disobedient unto the heavenly vision, but began to preach to Jews and Gentiles that they should repent and turn to God. Some old divine has said: "Every man is born with his back to God. Repentance is a change of one's course. It is right about face."

Sin is a turning away from God. As someone has said, it is aversion from God and conversion to the world: and true repentance means conversion to God and aversion from the world. When there is true contrition, the heart is broken for sin; when there is true conversion, the heart is broken from sin. We leave the old life, we are translated out of the kingdom of darkness into the kingdom of light. Wonderful, isn't it?

Unless our repentance includes this conversion, it is not worth much. If a man continues in sin, it is proof of an idle profession. It is like pumping away continually at the ship's pumps, without stopping the leaks. Solomon said: — "If they pray, and confess thy name, and turn from their sin . . ." Prayer and confession would be of no avail while they continued in sin. Let us heed God's call; let us forsake the old wicked way; let us return unto the Lord, and He will have mercy upon us; and to our God, for He will abundantly pardon.

If you have never turned to God, turn now. I have no sympathy with the idea that it takes six months, or six weeks, or six hours to be converted. It doesn't take you very long to turn around, does it? If you know you are wrong, then turn right about.

5. Confession of Christ

If you are converted, the next step is confess it openly. Listen: "If thou shalt confess with thy mouth the Lord Jesus Christ, and shalt believe in thine heart that God hath raised Him from the dead, thou shalt be saved. For with the heart man believeth unto righteousness, and with the mouth confession is made unto salvation."

Confession of Christ is the culmination of the work of true repentance. We owe it to the world, to our fellow-Christians, to ourselves. He died to redeem us, and shall we be ashamed or afraid to confess Him? Religion as an abstraction, as a doctrine, has little interest for the world, but what people can say from personal experience always has weight.

I remember some meetings being held in a locality where the tide did not rise very quickly, and bitter and reproachful things were being said about the work. But one day, one of the most prominent men in the place rose and said:

> "I want it to be known that I am a disciple of Jesus Christ; and if there is any odium to be cast on His cause, I am prepared to take my share of it."

It went through the meeting like an electric current, and a blessing came at once to his own soul and to the souls of others.

Men come to me and say: "Do you mean to affirm, Mr. Moody, that I've got to make a public confession when I accept Christ; do you mean to say I've got to confess Him in my place of business, and in my family? Am I to let the whole world know that I am on His side?"

That is precisely what I mean. A great many are willing to accept Christ, but they are not willing to publish it, to confess it. A great many are looking at the lions and the bears in the way. Now, my friends, the devil's mountains are only made of smoke. He can throw a straw into your path and make a mountain of it. He says to you: "You cannot confess and pray to your family; why, you'll break down! You cannot tell it to your shopmate; he will laugh at you." But when you accept Christ, you will have power to confess Him.

There was a young man in the West — it was the West in those days — who had been more or less interested about his soul's salvation. One afternoon, in his office, he said:

"I will accept Jesus Christ as my Lord and Savior."

He went home and told his wife (who was a nominal professor of religion) that he had made up his mind to serve Christ; and he added:

"After supper to-night I am going to take the company into the drawing-room, and erect the family altar."

"Well," said his wife, "you know some of the gentlemen who are coming to tea are skeptics, and they are older than you are, and don't you think you had better wait until after they have gone, or else go out in the kitchen and have your first prayer with the servants?"

The young man thought for a few moments, and then he said:

> "I have asked Jesus Christ into my house for the first time, and I shall take Him into the best room, not into the kitchen."

So he called his friends into the drawing room. There was a little sneering, but he read and prayed. That man afterwards became Chief Justice of the United States Court. Never be ashamed of the Gospel of Christ: it is the power of God unto salvation.

A young man enlisted, and was sent to his regiment. The first night he was in the barracks with about fifteen other young men who passed the time playing cards and gambling. Before retiring, he fell on his knees and prayed, and they began to curse him and jeer at him and throw boots at him.

So it went on the next night and the next, and finally the young man went and told the chaplain what had taken place, and asked what he should do.

"Well," said the chaplain, "you are not at home now, and the other men have just as much right in the barracks as you have. It makes them mad to hear you pray, and the Lord will hear you just as well if you say your prayers in bed and don't provoke them."

For weeks after the chaplain did not see the young man again, but one day he met him, and asked —

"By the way, did you take my advice?"

"I did, for two or three nights."

"How did it work?"

"Well," said the young man, "I felt like a whipped hound, and the third night I got out of bed, knelt down and prayed."

"Well," asked the chaplain, "how did that work?"

The young soldier answered: "We have a prayer-meeting there now every night, and three have been converted, and we are praying for the rest."

Oh, friends, I am so tired of weak Christianity. Let us be out and out for Christ; let us give no uncertain sound. If the world wants to call us fools, let them do it. It is only a little while; the crowning day is coming. Thank God for the privilege we have of confessing Christ.

Chapter 5

TRUE WISDOM

"They that be wise shall shine as the brightness of the firmament; and they that turn many to righteousness as the stars for ever and ever." Dan. 12:3.

That is the testimony of an old man, and one who had the richest and deepest experience of any man living on the face of the earth at the time. He was taken down to Babylon when a young man; some Bible students think he was not more than twenty years of age. If anyone had said, when this young Hebrew was carried away into captivity, that he would outrank all the mighty men of that day — that all the generals who had been victorious in almost every nation at that time were to be eclipsed by this young slave — probably no one would have believed it. Yet for five hundred years no man whose life is recorded in history shone as did this man. He outshone Nebuchadnezzar, Belshazzar, Cyrus, Darius, and all the princes and mighty monarchs of his day.

We are not told when he was converted to a knowledge of the true God, but I think we have good reason to believe that he had been brought under the influence of Jeremiah the prophet. Evidently some earnest, godly man, and no worldly professor, had made a deep impression upon him. Someone had at any rate taught him how he was to serve God.

We hear people nowadays talking about the hardness of the field where they labor; they say their position is a very peculiar one. Think of the field in which Daniel had to work. He was not only a slave, but he was held captive by a nation that detested the

Hebrews. The language was unknown to him. There he was among idolaters; yet he commenced at once to shine. He took his stand for God from the very first, and so he went on through his whole life. He gave the dew of his youth to God, and he continued faithful right on till his pilgrimage was ended.

Notice that all those who have made a deep impression on the world, and have shone most brightly have been men who lived in a dark day. Look at Joseph; he was sold as a slave into Egypt by the Ishmaelites; yet he took his God with him into captivity, as Daniel afterwards did. And he remained true to the last; he did not give up his faith because he had been taken away from home and placed among idolaters. He stood firm, and God stood by him.

Look at Moses who turned his back upon the gilded palaces of Egypt, and identified himself with his despised and down-trodden nation. If a man ever had a hard field it was Moses; yet he shone brightly, and never proved unfaithful to his God.

Elijah lived in a far darker day than we do. The whole nation was going over to idolatry. Ahab and his queen, and all the royal court were throwing their influence against the worship of the true God. Yet Elijah stood firm, and shone brightly in that dark and evil day. How his name stands out on the page of history!

Look at John the Baptist. I used to think I would like to live in the days of the prophets; but I have given up that idea. You may be sure that when a prophet appears on the scene, everything is dark, and the professing Church of God has gone over to the service of the god of this world. So it was when John the Baptist made his appearance. See how his name shines out today! Eighteen centuries have rolled away, and yet the fame of that wilderness preacher shines brighter than ever. He was looked down upon in his day and generation, but he has outlived all his enemies; his name will be revered and his work remembered as long as the Church is on the earth.

Talk about your field being a hard one! See how Paul shone for God as he went out, the first missionary to the heathen, telling them of the God whom he served, and who had sent His Son to die a cruel death in order to save the world. Men reviled him and his teachings; they laughed him to scorn when he spoke of the crucified One. But he went on preaching the Gospel of the Son of God. He was regarded as a poor tent-maker by the great and mighty ones of his day; but no one can now tell the name of any of his persecutors, or of those who lived at that time, unless their names happen to be associated with his, and they were brought into contact with him.

Now the fact is, all men like to shine. We may as well acknowledge it at once. Go into business circles, and see how men struggle to get into the front rank. Everyone wants to outshine his neighbor and to stand at the head of his profession. Go into the political world, and see how there is a struggle going on as to who shall be the greatest. If you go into a school, you find that there is a rivalry among the boys and girls. They all want to stand at the top of the class. When a boy does reach this position and outranks all the rest, the mother is very proud of it. She will manage to tell all the neighbors how Johnnie has got on, and what a number of prizes he has gained.

Go into the army and you find the same thing — one trying to outstrip the other; everyone is very anxious to shine and rise above his comrades. Go among the young men in their games, and see how anxious the one is to outdo the other. So we have all that desire in us; we like to shine above our fellows.

And yet there are very few who can really shine in the world. Once in a while one man will outstrip all his competitors. Every four years what a struggle goes on throughout our country as to who shall be the President of the United States, the battle raging for six months or a year. Yet only one man can get the prize. There are a good many struggling to get the place, but many are disappointed, because only one can attain the coveted prize. But in the kingdom of God the very least and the very weakest may shine if they will. Not only can one obtain the prize, but all may have it if they will.

It does not say in this passage that the statesmen are going to shine as the brightness of the firmament. The statesmen of Babylon are gone; their very names are forgotten.

It does not say that the nobility are going to shine. Earth's nobility are soon forgotten. John Bunyan, the Bedford tinker, has outlived the whole crowd of those who were the nobility in his day. They lived for self, and their memory is blotted out. He lived for God and for souls, and his name is as fragrant as ever it was.

We are not told that the merchants are going to shine. Who can tell the name of any of the millionaires of Daniel's day? They were all buried in oblivion a few years after their death. Who were the mighty conquerors of that day? But few can tell. It is true that we hear of Nebuchadnezzar, but probably we should not have known very much about him but of his relations to the prophet Daniel.

How different with this faithful prophet of the Lord! Twenty five centuries have passed away, and his name shines on, and on, and on, brighter and brighter. And it is going to shine while the Church of God exists. "They that be wise shall shine as the brightness of the firmament; and they that turn many to righteousness as the stars forever and ever."

How quickly the glory of this world fades away! Eighty years ago the great Napoleon almost made the earth to tremble. How he blazed and shone as an earthly warrior for a little while! A few years passed and a little island held that once proud and mighty conqueror; he died a poor broken-hearted prisoner. Where is he today? Almost forgotten. Who in all the world will say that Napoleon lives in their heart's affections?

But look at this despised and hated Hebrew prophet. They wanted to put him into the lions' den because he was too sanctimonious and too religious Yet see how green his memory is today! How his name is loved and honored for his faithfulness to his God.

Many years ago I was in Paris, at the time of the Great Exhibition. Napoleon the Third was then in his glory. Cheer after cheer would rise as he drove along the streets of the city. A few short years, and he fell from his lofty estate. He died an exile from his country and his throne, and where is his name today? Very few think about him at all, and if his name is mentioned it is not with love and esteem. How empty and short lived are the glory and the pride of this world! If we are wise, we will live for God and eternity; we will get outside of ourselves, and will care nothing for the honor and glory of this world. In Proverbs we read: "He that winneth souls is wise." If any man, woman, or child by a Godly life and example can win one soul to God, their life will not have been a failure. They will have outshone all the mighty men of their day, because they will have set a stream in motion that will flow on and on forever and ever.

God has left us down here to shine. We are not here to buy and sell and get gain, to accumulate wealth, to acquire worldly position. This earth, if we are Christians, is not our home; it is up yonder. God has sent us into the world to shine for Him — to light up this dark world. Christ came to be the Light of the world, but men put out that light. They took it to Calvary, and blew it out. Before Christ went up on high, He said to His disciples: "Ye are the light of the world. Ye are my witnesses. Go forth and carry the Gospel to the perishing nations of the earth."

So God has called us to shine, just as much as Daniel was sent into Babylon to shine. Let no man or woman say that they cannot shine because they have not so much influence as some others may have. What God wants you to do is to use the influence you have. Daniel probably did not have much influence down in Babylon at first, but God soon gave him more, because he was faithful and used what he had.

Remember a small light will do a good deal when it is in a very dark place. Put one little tallow candle in the middle of a large hall, and it will give a good deal of light.

Away out in the prairie regions, when meetings are held at night in the log schoolhouses, the announcement of the meeting is given out in this way:

"A meeting will be held by early candlelight."

The first man who comes brings a tallowdip with him. It is perhaps all he has; but he brings it, and sets it on the desk. It does not light the building much; but it is better than nothing at all. The next man brings his candle; and the next family bring theirs. By the time the house is full, there is plenty of light. So if we all shine a little, there will be a good deal of light. That is what God wants us to do. If we cannot all be lighthouses, any one of us can at any rate be a tallow candle.

A little light will sometimes do a great deal. The city of Chicago was set on fire by a cow kicking over a lamp, and a hundred thousand people were burnt out of house and home. Do not let Satan get the advantage of you, and make you think that because you cannot do any great thing you cannot do anything at all.

Then we must remember that we are to let our light shine. It does not say, "Make your light shine." You do not have to make light to shine; all you have to do is to let it shine.

I remember hearing of a man at sea who was very seasick. If there is a time when a man feels that he cannot do any work for the Lord it is then — in my opinion. While this man was sick, he heard that someone had fallen overboard. He was wondering if he could do anything to help to save the man. He laid hold of a light, and held it up to the port-hole. The drowning man was saved. When this man got over his attack of sickness, he went on deck one day and was talking with the man who was rescued. The saved man gave this testimony. He said he had gone down the second time, and was just going down again for the last time, when he put out his hand. Just then, he said, someone held a light at the port-hole, and the light fell on it. A sailor caught him by the hand and pulled him into the lifeboat.

It seemed a small thing to do to hold up the light; yet it saved the man's life. If you cannot do some great thing you can hold the light for some poor, perishing drunkard, who may be won to Christ and delivered from destruction. Let us take the torch of salvation and go into the dark homes, and hold up Christ to the people as the Savior of the world. If the perishing masses are to be reached, we must lay our lives right alongside theirs, and pray with them and labor for them. I would not give much for a man's Christianity if he is saved himself and is not willing to try and save others. It seems to me the basest ingratitude if we do not reach out the hand to others who are down in the same pit from which we were delivered. Who is able to reach and help drinking men like those who have themselves been slaves to the intoxicating cup? Will you not go out this very day and seek to rescue these men? If we were all to do what we can, we should soon empty the drinking saloons.

I remember reading of a blind man who was found sitting at

the corner of a street in a great city with a lantern beside him. Someone went up to him and asked what he had the lantern there for, seeing that he was blind, and the light was the same to him as the darkness. The blind man replied:

"I have it so that no one may stumble over me."

Dear friends, let us think of that. Where one man reads the Bible, a hundred read you and me. That is what Paul meant when he said we were to be living epistles of Christ, known and read of all men. I would not give much for all that can be done by sermons, if we do not preach Christ by our lives. If we do not commend the Gospel to people by our holy walk and conversation, we shall not win them to Christ. Some little act of kindness will perhaps do more to influence them than any number of long sermons.

A vessel was caught in a storm on Lake Erie, and they were trying to make for the harbor of Cleveland. At the entrance of that port they had what are called the upper lights and the lower lights. Away back on the bluffs were the upper lights burning brightly enough; but when they came near the harbor they could not see the lights showing the entrance to it. The pilot said he thought they had better get back on the lake again. The Captain said he was sure they would go down if they went back, and he urged the pilot to do what he could to gain the harbor. The pilot said there was very little hope of making the harbor, as he had nothing to guide him as to how he should steer the ship. They tried all they could to get her in. She rode on the top of the waves, and then into the trough of the sea, and at last they found themselves stranded on the beach, where the vessel was dashed to pieces. Someone had neglected the lower lights, and they had gone out.

Let us take warning. God keeps the upper lights burning as brightly as ever, but He has left us down here to keep the lower lights burning. We are to represent Him here, as Christ represents us up yonder. I sometimes think if we had as poor a representative in the courts above as God has down here on earth, we would have a pretty poor chance of heaven. Let us have our loins girt and our lights brightly burning, so that others may see the way and not walk in darkness.

Speaking of a lighthouse reminds me of what I heard about a man in the State of Minnesota, who, some years ago, was caught in a fearful storm. That State is cursed with storms which come sweeping down so suddenly in the winter time that escape is difficult. The snow will fall and the wind will beat it into the face of the traveler so that he cannot see two feet ahead. Many a man has been lost on the prairies when he has got caught in one of those storms.

This man was caught and was almost on the point of giving up, when he saw a little light in a log house. He managed to get there, and found a shelter from the fury of the tempest. He is now a wealthy man. As soon as he was able, he bought the farm, and built a beautiful house on the spot where the log building stood. On the top of a tower he put a revolving light, and every night when there comes a storm he lights it up in the hope that it may be the means of saving someone else.

That is true gratitude, and that is what God wants us to do. If He has rescued us and brought us up out of the horrible pit, let us be always looking to see if there is not someone else whom we can help to save.

I remember hearing of two men who had charge of a revolving light in a lighthouse on a rock-bound and stormy coast. Somehow the machinery went wrong, and the light did not revolve. They were so afraid that those at sea should mistake it for some other light, that they worked all the night through to keep the light moving round.

Let us keep our lights in the proper place, so that the world may see that the religion of Christ is not a sham but a reality. It is said that in the Grecian sports they had one game where the men ran with lights. They lit a torch at the altar, and ran a certain distance; sometimes they were on horseback. If a man came in with his light still burning, he received a prize; if his light had gone out, he lost the prize.

How many there are who, in their old age, have lost their light and their joy! They were once burning and shining lights in the family, in the Sunday-school, and in the Church. But something has come in between them and God — the world or self — and their light has gone out. Reader, if you are one who has had this experience, may God help you to come back to the altar of the Savior's love and light up your torch anew, so that you can go out into the lanes and alleys, and let the light of the Gospel shine in these dark homes.

As I have already said, if we only lead one soul to Jesus Christ we may set a stream in motion that will flow on when we are dead and gone. Away up the mountain side there is a little spring; it seems so small that an ox might drink it up at a draught. By and by it becomes a rivulet; other rivulets run into it. Before long it is a large brook, and then it becomes a broad river sweeping onward to the sea. On its banks are cities, towns and villages, where many thousands live. Vegetation flourishes on every side, and commerce is carried down its stately bosom to distant lands.

So if you turn one to Christ, that one may turn a hundred; they may turn a thousand, and so the stream, small at first, goes on broadening and deepening as it rolls toward eternity.

In the book of Revelation we read: "I heard a voice from heaven saying unto me, Write, Blessed are the dead which die in the Lord from henceforth: yea, saith the Spirit, that they may rest from their labors; and their works do follow them."

There are many mentioned in the Scriptures of whom we read that they lived so many years and then they died. The cradle and the grave are brought close together; they lived and they died, and that is all we know about them. So in these days you could write on the tombstone of a great many professing Christians that they were born on such a day and they died on such a day; there is nothing whatever between.

But there is one thing you cannot bury with a good man; his influence still lives. They have not buried Daniel yet: his influence is as great today as it ever was. Do you tell me that Joseph is dead? His influence still lives and will continue to live on and on. You may bury the frail tenement of clay that a good man lives in, but you cannot get rid of his influence and example. Paul was never more powerful than he is today.

Do you tell me that John Howard, who went into so many of the dark prisons in Europe, is dead? Is Henry Martyn, or Wilberforce, or John Bunyan dead? Go into the Southern States, and there you will find millions of men and women who once were slaves. Mention to any of them the name of Wilberforce, and see how quickly the eye will light up. He lived for something else besides himself, and his memory will never die out of the hearts of those for whom he lived and labored.

Is Wesley or Whitefield dead? The names of those great evangelists were never more honored than they are now. Is John Knox dead? You can go to any part of Scotland today, and feel the power of his influence.

I will tell you who are dead. The enemies of these servants of God — those who persecuted them and told lies about them. But the men themselves have outlived all the lies that were uttered concerning them. Not only that; they will shine in another world. How true are the words of the old Book: "They that be wise shall shine as the brightness of the firmament; and they that turn many to righteousness as the stars forever and ever."

Let us go on turning as many as we can to righteousness. Let us be dead to the world, to its lies, its pleasures, and its ambitions. Let us live for God, continually going forth to win souls for Him.

Let me quote a few words by Dr. Chalmers: "Thousands of men breathe, move and live, pass off the stage of life, and are heard no more — Why? They do not partake of good in the world, and none were blessed by them; none could point to them as the means of their redemption; not a line they wrote, not a word they spoke could be recalled; and so they perished; their light went out in darkness, and they were not remembered more than insects of yesterday. Will you thus live and die, O man immortal? Live for something. Do good, and leave behind you a monument of virtue that the storms of time can never destroy. Write your name in kindness, love and mercy, on the hearts of the thousands you come in contact with year by year; you will never be forgotten. No, your name, your deeds will be as legible on the hearts you leave behind as the stars on the brow of evening. Good deeds will shine as the stars of heaven."

Chapter 6

"COME THOU AND ALL THY HOUSE INTO THE ARK"

I want to call your attention to a text that you will find in the seventh chapter of Genesis, first verse. When God speaks, you and I can afford to listen. It is not man speaking now, but it is God. "The Lord said unto Noah, Come thou and all thy house into the ark."

Perhaps some sceptic is reading this, and perhaps some church member will join with him and say,

"I hope Mr. Moody is not going to preach about the ark. I thought that was given up by all intelligent people."

But I want to say that I haven't given it up. When I do, I am going to give up the whole Bible. There is hardly any portion of the Old Testament Scripture but that the Son of God set His seal to it when He was down here in the world.

Men say, "I don't believe in the story of the flood."

Christ connected His own return to this world with that flood: "And as it was in the days of Noah, so shall it be also in the days of the Son of man. They did eat, they drank, they married wives, they were given in marriage, until the day that Noah entered into the ark, and the flood came, and destroyed them all."

I believe the story of the flood just as much as I do the third chapter of John. I pity any man that is picking the old Book to pieces. The moment that we give up any one of these things, we touch the deity of the Son of God. I have noticed that when a man does begin to pick the Bible to pieces, it doesn't take him long to tear it all to pieces. What is the use of being five years about what you can do in five minutes?

A Solemn Message

One hundred and twenty years before God spake the words of my text, Noah had received the most awful communication that ever came from heaven to earth. No man up to that time, and I think no man since, has ever received such a communication. God said that on account of the wickedness of the world He was going to destroy the world by water. We can have no idea of the extent and character of that antediluvian wickedness. The Bible piles one expression on another, in its effort to emphasize it. "God saw that the wickedness of man was great in the earth, and that every imagination of the thoughts of his heart was only evil continually. And it repented the Lord that He had made man on the earth, and it grieved him at His heart. . . . The earth also was corrupt before God, and the earth was filled with violence. And God looked upon the earth, and, behold, it was corrupt; for all flesh had corrupted his way upon the earth." Men lived five hundred years and more then, and they had time to mature in their sins.

How the Message was Received

For one hundred and twenty years God strove with those antediluvians. He never smites without warning, and they had their warning. Every time Noah drove a nail into the ark it was a warning to them. Every sound of the hammer echoed, "I believe in God." If they had repented and cried as they did at Nineveh, I believe God would have heard their cry and spared them. But there was no cry for mercy. I have no doubt but that they ridiculed the idea that God was going to destroy the world. I have no doubt but that there were atheists who said there was not any God anyhow. I got hold of one of them some time ago. I said,

"How do you account for the formation of the world?"

"Oh! force and matter work together, and by chance the world was created."

I said, "It is a singular thing that your tongue isn't on the top of your head if force and matter just threw it together in that manner."

If I should take out my watch and say that force and matter worked together, and out came the watch, you would say I was a lunatic of the first order. Wouldn't you? And yet they say that this old world was made by chance! "It threw itself together!"

I met a man in Scotland, and he took the ground that there was no God. I asked him,

"How do you account for creation, for all these rocks?" (They have a great many rocks in Scotland.)

"Why!" he said, "any school boy could account for that."

"Well, how was the first rock made?"

"Out of sand."

"How was the first sand made?"

"Out of rock."

You see he had it all arranged so nicely. Sand and rock, rock and sand. I have no doubt but that Noah had these men to contend with.

Then there was a class called agnostics, and there are a good many of their grandchildren, alive today. Then there was another class who said they believed there was a God; they couldn't make themselves believe that the world happened by chance; but God was too merciful to punish sin. He was so full of compassion and love that He couldn't punish sin. The drunkard, the harlot, the gambler, the murderer, the thief and the libertine would all share alike with the saints at the end. Supposing the governor of your state was so tender-hearted that he could not bear to have a man suffer, could not bear to see a man put in jail, and he should go and set all the prisoners free. How long would he be governor? You would have him out of office before the sun set. These very men that talk about God's mercy, would be the first to raise a cry against a governor who would not have a man put in prison when he had done wrong.

Then another class took the ground that God could not destroy the world anyway. They might have a great flood which would rise up to the meadowlands and lowlands, but all it would be necessary to do would be to go up on the hills and mountains. That would be a hundred times better than Noah's ark. Or if it should come to that, they could build rafts, which would be a good deal better than that ark. They had never seen such an ugly looking thing. It was about five hundred feet long, and about eighty feet wide, and fifty feet high. It had three stories, and only one small window.

And then, I suppose there was a large class who took the ground that Noah must be wrong because he was in such a minority. That is a great argument now, you know. Noah was greatly in the minority. But he went on working.

If they had saloons then, and I don't doubt but that they had, for we read that there was "violence in the land," and wherever you have alcohol you have violence. We read also that Noah planted a vineyard and fell into the sin of intemperance. He was a righteous man, and if he did that, what must the others have done? Well, if they had saloons, no doubt they sang ribald songs about Noah and his ark, and if they had theaters they likely acted it out, and mothers took their children to see it.

And if they had the press in those days, every now and then there would appear a skit about "Noah and his folly." Reporters would come and interview him, and if they had an Associated Press, every few days a dispatch would be sent out telling how the work on the ark was progressing.

And perhaps they had excursions, and offered as an inducement that people could go through the ark. And if Noah happened to be around they would nudge each other and say:

"That's Noah. Don't you think there is a strange look in his eye?"

As a Scotchman would say, they thought him a little daft. Thank God a man can afford to be mad. A mad man thinks everyone else mad but himself A drunkard does not call himself mad when he is drinking up all his means. Those men who stand and deal out death and damnation to men are not called mad; but a man is called mad when he gets into the ark, and is saved for time and eternity. And I expect if the word crank was in use, they called Noah "an old crank."

And so all manner of sport was made of Noah and his ark. And the business men went on buying and selling, while Noah went on preaching and toiling. They perhaps had some astronomers, and they were gazing up at the stars, and saying, "Don't you be concerned. There is no sign of a coming storm in the heavens. We are very wise men, and if there was a storm coming, we should read it in the heavens." And they had geologists digging away, and they said, "There is no sign in the earth." Even the carpenters who helped build the ark might have made fun of him, but they were like lots of people at the present day, who will help build a church, and perhaps give money for its support, but will never enter it themselves.

Well, things went on as usual. Little lambs skipped on the hillsides each spring. Men sought after wealth, and if they had leases, I expect they ran for longer periods than ours do. We think ninety-nine years a long time, but I don't doubt but that theirs ran for nine hundred and ninety nine years. And when they came to sign a lease they would say with a twinkle in their eyes:

"Why, this old Noah says the world is coming to an end in one hundred and twenty years, and it's twenty years since he started the story. But I guess I will sign the lease and risk it."

Someone has said that Noah must have been deaf, or he could not have stood the jeers and sneers of his countrymen. But if he was deaf to the voice of men, he heard the voice of God when He told him to build the ark.

I can imagine one hundred years have rolled away, and the work on the ark ceases. Men say, "What has he stopped work for?" He has gone on a preaching tour, to tell the people of the coming storm — that God is going to sweep every man from the face of the earth unless he is in the ark. But he cannot get a man to believe him except his own family. Some of the old men have passed away, and they died saying: "Noah is wrong." Poor Noah! He must have had a hard time of it. I don't think I should have had the grace to work for one hundred and twenty years without a convert. But he just toiled on, believing the word of God.

And now the hundred and twenty years are up. In the spring of the year Noah did not plant anything, for he knew the flood was coming, and the people say: "Every year before he has planted, but this year he thinks the world is going to be destroyed, and he hasn't planted anything."

Moving in

But I can imagine one beautiful morning, not a cloud to be seen, Noah has got his communication. He has heard the voice that he heard one hundred and twenty years before — the same old voice. Perhaps there had been silence for one hundred and twenty years. But the voice rang through his soul once again, "Noah, come thou and all thy house into the ark."

The word "come" occurs about nineteen hundred times in the Bible, it is said, and this is the first time. It meant salvation. You can see Noah and all his family moving into the ark. They are bringing the household furniture.

Some of his neighbors say, "Noah, what is your hurry? you will have plenty of time to get into that old ark. What is your hurry? There are no windows and you cannot look out to see when the storm is coming." But he heard the voice and obeyed.

Some of his relatives might have said, "What are you going to do with the old homestead?"

Noah says, "I don't want it. The storm is coming." He tells them the day of grace is closing, that worldly wealth is of no value, and that the ark is the only place of safety. We must bear in mind that these railroads that we think so much of, will soon go down; they only run for time, not for eternity. The heavens will be on fire, and then what will property, honor, and position in society be worth?

The first thing that alarms them is, they rise one morning, and lo! the heavens are filled with the fowls of the air. They are flying into the ark, two by two. They come from the desert; they come from the mountain; they come from all parts of the world. They are going into the ark. It must have been a strange sight. I can hear the people cry, "Great God! what is the meaning of this?" And they look down on the earth; and, with great alarm and surprise, they see little insects creeping up two by two, coming from all parts of the world. Then behold! there come cattle and beasts, two by two. The neighbors cry out, "What does this mean?" They run to their statesmen and wise men, who have told them there was no sign of a coming storm, and ask them why it is that those birds, animals, and creeping things go toward the ark, as if guided by some unseen hand.

"Well," the statesmen and wise men say, "We cannot explain it; but give yourselves no trouble; God is not going to destroy the world. Business was never better than it is now. Do you think if God was going to destroy the world, He would let us go on so prosperously as He has? There is no sign of a coming storm. What has made these creeping insects and these wild beasts of the forest go into the ark, we do not know. We cannot understand it; it is very strange. But there is no sign of anything going to happen. The stars are bright, and the sun shines as bright as ever it did. Everything moves on as it has been moving for all time past. You can hear the children playing in the street. You can hear the voice of the bride and bridegroom in the land, and all is merry as ever."

I imagine the alarm passed away, and they fell into their regular courses. Noah comes out and says: "The door is going to be shut. Come in. God is going to destroy the world. See the animals, how they have come up. The communication has come to them direct from heaven." But the people only mocked on.

Do you know, when the hundred and twenty years were up, God gave the world seven days' grace? Did you ever notice that? If there had been a cry during those seven days, I believe it would have been heard. But there was none.

At length the last day had come, the last hour, the last minute, ay! the last second. God Almighty came down and shut the door of that ark. No angel, no man, but God Himself shut that door, and when once the master of the house has risen and shut to the door, the doom of the world is sealed; and the doom of that old world was forever sealed. The sun had gone down upon the glory of that old world for the last time. You can hear away off in the distance the mutterings of the storm. You can hear the thunder rolling. The lightning begins to flash, and the old world reels. The storm bursts upon them, and that old ark of Noah's would have been worth more than the whole world to them.

I want to say to any scoffer who reads this, that you can laugh at the Bible, you can scoff at your mother's God, you can laugh at ministers and Christians, but the hour is coming when one promise in that old Book will be worth more to you than ten thousand worlds like this.

The windows of heaven are opened and the fountains of the great deep are broken up. The waters come bubbling up, and the sea bursts its bounds and leaps over its walls. The rivers begin to swell. The people living in the lowlands flee to the mountains and highlands. They flee up the hillsides. And there is a wail going up:

"Noah! Noah! Noah! Let us in."

They leave their homes and come to the ark now. They pound on the ark. Hear them cry:

"Noah! Let us in. Noah! Have mercy on us."

"I am your nephew."

"I am your niece."

"I am your uncle."

Ah, there is a voice inside, saying: "I would like to let you in; but God has shut the door, and I cannot open it!"

God shut that door! When the door is shut, there is no hope. Their cry for mercy was too late; their day of grace was closed. Their last hour had come. God had plead with them; God had invited them to come in; but they had mocked at the invitation. They scoffed and ridiculed the idea of a deluge. Now it is too late.

God did not permit anyone to survive to tell us how they perished. When Job lost his family, there came a messenger to him: but there came no messenger from the antediluvians; not even Noah himself could see the world perish. If he could, he would have seen men and women and children dashing against that ark; the waves rising higher and higher, while those outside were perishing, dying in unbelief. Some think to escape by climbing the trees, and think the storm will soon go down; but it rains on, day and night, for forty days and forty nights, and they are swept away as the waves dash against them. The statesmen and astronomers and great men call for mercy; but it is too late. They had disobeyed the God of mercy. He had called, and they refused. He had plead with them, but they had laughed and mocked. But now the time is come for judgment instead of mercy.

Judgment

The time is coming again when God will deal in judgment with the world. It is but a little while; we know not when, but it is sure to come. God's word has gone forth that this world shall be rolled together like a scroll, and shall be on fire. What then will become of your soul? It is a loving call, "Now come, thou and all thy house, into the ark." Twenty four hours before the rain began to fall, Noah's ark, if it had been sold at auction, would not have brought as much as it would be worth for kindling wood. But twenty four hours after the rain began to fall, Noah's ark was worth more than all the world. There was not then a man living but would have given all he was worth for a seat in the ark. You may turn away and laugh.

"I believe in Christ!" you say; "I would rather be without Him than have Him."

But bear in mind, the time is coming when Christ will be worth more to you than ten thousand worlds like this. Bear in mind that He is offered to you now. This is a day of grace; it is a day of mercy. You will find, if you read your Bible carefully, that God always precedes judgment with grace. Grace is a forerunner of judgment. He called these men in the days of Noah in love. They would have been saved if they had repented in those one hundred and twenty years. When Christ came to plead with the people in Jerusalem, it was their day of grace; but they mocked and laughed at Him. He said: "O Jerusalem, Jerusalem, thou that killest the prophets, and stonest them which are sent unto thee, how often would I have gathered thy children together, even as a hen gathereth her chickens under her wings, and ye would not!" Forty years afterward, thousands of the people begged that their lives might be spared; and eleven hundred thousand perished in that city.

In 1857 a revival swept over this country in the east and on to the western cities, clear over to the Pacific coast. It was God calling the nation to Himself. Half a million people united with the Church at that time. Then the war broke out. We were baptized with the Holy Ghost in 1857, and in 1861 we were baptized in blood. It was a call of mercy, preceding judgment.

Are Your Children Safe?

The text which I have selected has a special application to Christian people and to parents. This command of the Scripture was given to Noah not only for his own safety, but that of his household, and the question which I put to each father and mother is this: "Are your children in the ark of God?" You may scoff at it, but it is a very important question. Are all your children in? Are all your grandchildren in? Don't rest day or night until you get your children in. I believe my children have fifty temptations where I had one. I am one of those who believe that in the great cities there is a snare set upon the corner of every street for our sons and daughters; and I don't believe it is our business to spend our time in accumulating bonds and stocks. Have I done all I can to get my children in? That is it.

Now, let me ask another question: What would have been Noah's feelings if, when God called him into the ark, his children would not have gone with him? If he had lived such a false life that his children had no faith in his word, what would have been his feelings? He would have said: "There is my poor boy on the mountain. Would to God I had died in his place! I would rather have perished than had him perish." David cried over his son: "Oh, my son Absalom, my son, my son Absalom, would God I had died for thee!" Noah loved his children, and they had confidence in him.

Someone sent me a paper a number of years ago, containing an article that was marked. Its title was: "Are all the children in?" An old wife lay dying. She was nearly one hundred years of age, and the husband who had taken the journey with her, sat by her side. She was just breathing faintly, but suddenly she revived, opened her eyes, and said:

"Why! it is dark."

"Yes, Janet, it is dark."

"Is it night?"

"Oh, yes! it is midnight."

"Are all the children in?"

There was that old mother living life over again. Her youngest child had been in the grave twenty years, but she was traveling back into the old days, and she fell asleep in Christ asking, "Are all the children in?"

Dear friend, are they all in? Put the question to yourself now. Is John in? Is James in? Or is he immersed in business and pleasure? Is he living a double and dishonest life? Say! where is your boy, mother? Where is your son, your daughter? Is it well with your children? Can you say it is?

After being superintendent of a Sunday school in Chicago for a number of years, a school of over a thousand members, children that came from godless homes, having mothers and fathers working against me, taking the children off on excursions on Sunday, and doing all they could to break up the work I was trying to do, I used to think that if I should ever stand before an audience I would speak to no one but parents; that would be my chief business. It is an old saying — "Get the lamb, and you will get the sheep." I gave that up years ago. Give me the sheep, and then I will have someone to nurse the lamb; but get a lamb and convert him, and if he has a godless father and mother, you will have little chance with that child. What we want is godly homes. The home was established long before the Church.

I have no sympathy with the idea that our children have to grow up before they are converted. Once I saw a lady with three daughters at her side, and I stepped up to her and asked her if she was a Christian.

"Yes, sir."

Then I asked the oldest daughter if she was a Christian. The chin began to quiver, and the tears came into her eyes, and she said,

"I wish I was."

The mother looked very angrily at me and said, "I don't want you to speak to my children on that subject. They don't understand." And in great rage she took them all away from me. One daughter was fourteen years old, one twelve, and the other ten, but they were not old enough to be talked to about religion. Let them drift into the world and plunge into worldly amusements, and then see how hard it is to reach them. Many a mother is mourning today because her boy has gone beyond her reach, and will not allow her to pray with him. She may pray for him, but he will not let her pray or talk with him. In those early days when his mind was tender and young, she might have led him to Christ. Bring them in. "Suffer the little children to come unto Me." Is there a prayerless father reading this? May God let the arrow go down into your soul! Make up your mind that, God helping you, you will get the children in. God's order is to the father first, but if he isn't true to his duty, then the mother should be true, and save the children from the wreck. Now is the time to do it while you have them under your roof. Exert your parental influence over them.

I never speak to parents but I think of two fathers, one of whom lived on the banks of the Mississippi, the other in New York. The first one devoted all his time to amassing wealth. He had a son to whom he was much attached, and one day the boy was brought home badly injured. The father was informed that the boy could live but a short time, and he broke the news to his son as gently as possible.

"You say I cannot live, father? O! then pray for my soul," said the boy.

In all those years that father had never said a prayer for that boy, and he told him he couldn't. Shortly after, the boy died. That father has said since that he would give all that he possessed if he could call that boy back only to offer one short prayer for him.

The other father had a boy who had been sick some time, and he came home one day and found his wife weeping. She said:

"I cannot help but believe that this is going to prove fatal."

The man started, and said: "If you think so, I wish you would tell him."

But the mother could not tell her boy. The father went to the sick room, and he saw that death was feeling for the cords of life, and he said:

"My son, do you know you are not going to live?"

The little fellow looked up and said: "No; is this death that I feel stealing over me? Will I die today?"

"Yes, my son, you cannot live the day out."

And the little fellow smiled and said: "Well, father, I shall be with Jesus tonight, shan't I?"

"Yes, you will spend the night with the Lord," and the father broke down and wept.

The little fellow saw the tears, and said: "Don't weep for me. I will go to Jesus and tell Him that ever since I can remember you have prayed for me."

I have three children, and if God should take them from me, I would rather have them take such a message home to Him than to have the wealth of the whole world. Oh! would to God I could say something to stir you, fathers and mothers, to get your children into the ark.

Chapter 7

HUMILITY

"*Learn of me, for I am meek and lowly in heart.*" — Matthew 11:29.

There is no harder lesson to learn than the lesson of humility. It is not taught in the schools of men, only in the school of Christ. It is the rarest of all the gifts. Very rarely do we find a man or woman who is following closely the footsteps of the Master in meekness and in humility. I believe that it is the hardest lesson which Jesus Christ had to teach His disciples while He was here upon earth. It almost looked at first as though He had failed to teach it to the twelve men who had been with Him almost constantly for three years.

I believe that if we are humble enough we shall be sure to get a great blessing. After all, I think that more depends upon us than upon the Lord, because He is always ready to give a blessing and give it freely, but we are not always in a position to receive it. He always blesses the humble, and, if we can get down in the dust before Him, no one will go away disappointed. It was Mary at the feet of Jesus, who had chosen the "better part."

Did you ever notice the reason Christ gave for learning of Him? He might have said: "Learn of me, because I am the most advanced thinker of the age. I have performed miracles that no man else has performed. I have shown my supernatural power in a thousand ways." But no: the reason He gave was that He was "meek, and lowly in heart."

We read of the three men in Scripture whose faces shone, and all three were noted for their meekness and humility. We are told that the face of Christ shone at His transfiguration; Moses, after he had been in the mount for forty days, came down from his communion with God with a shining face; and when Stephen stood before the Sanhedrim on the day of his death, his face was lighted up with glory. If our faces are to shine we must get into the valley of humility; we must go down in the dust before God.

Bunyan says that it is hard to get down into the valley of humiliation, the descent into it is steep and rugged; but that it is very fruitful and fertile and beautiful when once we get there. I think that no one will dispute that; almost every man, even the ungodly, admires meekness.

Someone asked Augustine, what was the first of the religious graces, and he said, "Humility." They asked him what was the second, and he replied, "Humility." They asked him the third, and he said, "Humility." I think that if we are humble, we have all the graces.

Some years ago I saw what is called a sensitive plant. I happened to breathe on it, and suddenly it drooped its head; I touched it, and it withered away. Humility is as sensitive as that; it cannot safely be brought out on exhibition. A man who is flattering himself that he is humble and is walking close to the Master, is self-deceived. It consists not in thinking meanly of ourselves, but in not thinking of ourselves at all. Moses wist not that his face shone. If humility speaks of itself, it is gone.

Someone has said that the grass is an illustration of this lowly grace. It was created for the lowliest service. Cut it, and it springs up again. The cattle feed upon it, and yet how beautiful it is.

The showers fall upon the mountain peaks, and very often leave them barren because they rush down into the meadows and valleys and make the lowly places fertile. If a man is proud and lifted up, rivers of grace may flow over him and yet leave him barren and unfruitful, while they bring blessing to the man who has been brought low by the grace of God.

A man can counterfeit love, he can counterfeit faith, he can counterfeit hope and all the other graces, but it is very difficult to counterfeit humility. You soon detect mock humility. They have a saying in the East among the Arabs, that as the tares and the wheat grow they show which God has blessed. The ears that God has blessed bow their heads and acknowledge every grain, and the more fruitful they are the lower their heads are bowed. The tares which God has sent as a curse, lift up their heads erect, high above the wheat, but they are only fruitful of evil. I have a pear tree on my farm which is very beautiful; it appears to be one of the most beautiful trees on my place. Every branch seems to be reaching up to the light and stands almost like a wax candle, but I never get any fruit from it. I have another tree, which was so full of fruit last year that the branches almost touched the ground. If we only get down low enough, my friends, God will use every one of us to His glory.

"As the lark that soars the highest builds her nest the lowest; as the nightingale that sings so sweetly, sings in the shade when all things rest; as the branches that are most laden with fruit, bend lowest; as the ship most laden, sinks deepest in the water; — so the holiest Christians are the humblest."

The London Times some years ago told the story of a petition that was being circulated for signatures. It was a time of great excitement, and this petition was intended to have great influence in the House of Lords; but there was one word left out. Instead of reading, "We humbly beseech thee," it read, "We beseech thee." So it was ruled out. My friends, if we want to make an appeal to the God of Heaven, we must humble ourselves; and if we do humble ourselves before the Lord, we shall not be disappointed.

As I have been studying some Bible characters that illustrate humility, I have been ashamed of myself. If you have any regard for me, pray that I may have humility. When I put my life beside the life of some of these men, I say, Shame on the Christianity of the present day. If you want to get a good idea of yourself, look at some of the Bible characters that have been clothed with meekness and humility, and see what a contrast is your position before God and man.

One of the meekest characters in history was John the Baptist. You remember when they sent a deputation to him and asked if he was Elias, or this prophet, or that prophet, he said, "No." Now he might have said some very flattering things of himself. He might have said:

> "I am the son of the old priest Zacharias. Haven't you heard of my fame as a preacher? I have baptized more people probably, than any man living. The world has never seen a preacher like myself."

I honestly believe that in the present day most men standing in his position would do that. On the railroad train, some time ago, I heard a man talking so loud that all the people in the car could hear him. He said that he had baptized more people than any man in his denomination. He told how many thousand miles he had traveled, how many sermons he had preached, how many open-air services he had held, and this and that, until I was so ashamed that I had to hide my head. This is the age of boasting. It is the day of the great "I."

My attention was recently called to the fact that in all the Psalms you cannot find any place where David refers to his victory over the giant, Goliath. If it had been in the present day, there would have been a volume written about it at once; I don't know how many poems there would be telling of the great things that this man had done. He would have been in demand as a lecturer, and would have added a title to his name: G. G. K., — Great Giant Killer. That is how it is today: great evangelists, great preachers, great theologians, great bishops.

"John," they asked, "who are you?"

"I am nobody. I am to be heard, not to be seen. I am only a voice."

He hadn't a word to say about himself. I once heard a little bird faintly singing close by me, — at last it got clear out of sight, and then its notes were still sweeter. The higher it flew the sweeter sounded its notes. If we can only get self out of sight and learn of Him who was meek and lowly in heart we shall be lifted up into heavenly places.

Mark tells us, in the first chapter and seventh verse, that John came and preached saying, "There cometh one mightier than I after me, the latchet of whose shoes I am not worthy to stoop down and unloose." Think of that; and bear in mind that Christ was looked upon as a deceiver, a village carpenter, and yet here is John, the son of the old priest, who had a much higher position in the sight of men than that of Jesus. Great crowds were coming to hear him, and even Herod attended his meetings.

When his disciples came and told John that Christ was beginning to draw crowds, he nobly answered: "A man can receive nothing, except it be given him from heaven. Ye yourselves bear me witness that I said, I am not the Christ, but that I am sent before Him. He that hath the bride is the bridegroom: but the friend of the bridegroom, which standeth and heareth him, rejoiceth greatly because of the bridegroom's voice: this my joy therefore is fulfilled. He must increase, but I must decrease."

It is easy to read that, but it is hard for us to live in the power of it. It is very hard for us to be ready to decrease, to grow smaller and smaller, that Christ may increase. The morning star fades away when the sun rises.

"He that cometh from above is above all: he that is of the earth is earthly, and speaketh of the earth: He that cometh from heaven is above all, and what He hath seen and heard, that He testifieth; and no man receiveth His testimony. He that hath received His testimony hath set to his seal that God is true. For He whom God hath sent speaketh the words of God: for God giveth not the Spirit by measure unto Him."

Let us now turn the light upon ourselves. Have we been decreasing of late? Do we think less of ourselves and of our position than we did a year ago? Are we seeking to obtain some position of dignity? Are we wanting to hold on to some title, and are we offended because we are not treated with the courtesy that we think is due us? Some time ago I heard a man in the pulpit say that he should take offence if he was not addressed by his title. My dear friend, are you going to take that position that you must have a title, and that you must have every letter addressed with that title or you will be offended? John did not want any title, and when we are right with God, we shall not be caring about titles. In one of his early epistles Paul calls himself the "least of all the apostles."

Later on he claims to be "less than the least of all saints," and again, just before his death, humbly declares that he is the "chief of sinners." Notice how he seems to have grown smaller and smaller in his own estimation. So it was with John. And I do hope and pray that as the days go by we may feel like hiding ourselves, and let God have all the honor and glory.

"When I look back upon my own religious experience," says Andrew Murray, "or round upon the Church of Christ in the world, I stand amazed at the thought of how little humility is sought after as the distinguishing feature of the discipleship of Jesus. In preaching and living, in the daily intercourse of the home and social life, in the more special fellowship with Christians, in the direction and performance of work for Christ — alas! how much proof there is that humility is not esteemed the cardinal virtue, the only root from which the graces can grow, the one indispensable condition of true fellowship with Jesus."

See what Christ says about John. "He was a burning and shining light." Christ gave him the honor that belonged to him. If you take a humble position, Christ will see it. If you want God to help you, then take a low position.

I am afraid that if we had been in John's place, many of us would have said: "What did Christ say, — I am a burning and shining light?" Then we would have had that recommendation put in the newspapers, and would have sent them to our friends, with that part marked in blue pencil. Sometimes I get a letter just full of clippings from the newspapers, stating that this man is more eloquent than Gough, etc. And the man wants me to get him some church. Do you think that a man who has such eloquence would be looking for a church? No, they would all be looking for him.

My dear friends, isn't it humiliating? Sometimes I think it is a wonder that any man is converted these days. Let another praise you. Don't be around praising yourself. If we want God to lift us up, let us get down. The lower we get, the higher God will lift us. It is Christ's eulogy of John, "Greater than any man born of woman."

There is a story told of Carey, the great missionary, that he was invited by the Governor-general of India to go to a dinner party at which were some military officers belonging to the aristocracy, and who looked down upon missionaries with scorn and contempt.

One of these officers said at the table: "I believe that Carey was a shoemaker, wasn't he, before he took up the profession of a missionary?"

Mr. Carey spoke up and said: "Oh no, I was only a cobbler. I could mend shoes, and wasn't ashamed of it."

The one prominent virtue of Christ, next to His obedience, is His humility; and even His obedience grew out of His humility. Being in the form of God, He counted it not a thing to be grasped to be on an equality with God, but He emptied Himself, taking the form of a bond-servant, and was made in the likeness of men. And being found in fashion as a man, He humbled Himself, and became obedient unto death, yea, the death of the cross. In His lowly birth, His submission to His earthly parents, His seclusion during thirty years, His consorting with the poor and despised, His entire submission and dependence upon His Father, this virtue that was consummated in His death on the cross, shines out.

One day Jesus was on His way to Capernaum, and was talking about His coming death and suffering, and about His resurrection, and He heard quite a heated discussion going on behind Him. When He came into the house at Capernaum, He turned to His disciples, and said:

"What was all that discussion about?"

I see John look at James, and Peter at Andrew, — and they all looked ashamed. "Who shall be the greater?" That discussion has wrecked party after party, one society after another — "Who shall be the greatest?"

The way Christ took to teach them humility was by putting a little child in their midst and saying: "If you want to be great, take that little child for an example, and he who wants to be the greatest, let him be servant of all."

To me, one of the saddest things in all the life of Jesus Christ was the fact that just before His crucifixion, His disciples should have been striving to see who should be the greatest, that night He instituted the Supper, and they ate the Passover together. It was His last night on earth, and they never saw Him so sorrowful before. He knew Judas was going to sell Him for thirty pieces of silver. He knew that Peter would deny Him. And yet, in addition to this, when going into the very shadow of the cross, there arose this strife as to who should be the greatest. He took a towel and girded Himself like a slave, and He took a basin of water and stooped and washed their feet. That was another object lesson of humility. He said, "Ye call me Lord, and ye do well. If you want to be great in my Kingdom, be servant of all. If you serve, you shall be great."

When the Holy Ghost came, and those men were filled, from that time on mark the difference: Matthew takes up his pen to write, and he keeps Matthew out of sight. He tells what Peter and Andrew did, but he calls himself Matthew "the publican." He tells how they left all to follow Christ, but does not mention the feast he gave. Jerome says that Mark's gospel is to be regarded as memoirs of Peter's discourses, and to have been published by his authority. Yet here we constantly find that damaging things are mentioned about Peter, and things to his credit are not referred to. Mark's gospel omits all allusion to Peter's faith in venturing on the sea, but goes into detail about the story of his fall and denial of our Lord. Peter put himself down, and lifted others up.

If the Gospel of Luke had been written today, it would be signed by the great Dr. Luke, and you would have his photograph as a frontispiece. But you can't find Luke's name; he keeps out of sight. He wrote two books, and his name is not to be found in either. John covers himself always under the expression — "the disciple whom Jesus loved." None of the four men whom history and tradition assert to be the authors of the gospels, lay claim to the authorship in their writings. Dear man of God, I would that I had the same spirit, that I could just get out of sight, — hide myself.

My dear friends, I believe our only hope is to be filled with the Spirit of Christ. May God fill us, so that we shall be filled with meekness and humility. Let us take the hymn, "O, to be nothing, nothing," and make it the language of our hearts. It breathes the spirit of Him who said: "The Son can do nothing of Himself!"

Oh to be nothing, nothing!
Only to lie at His feet,
A broken and emptied vessel,
For the Master's use made meet.
Emptied, that He might fill me
As forth to His service I go;
Broken, that so unhindered,
His life through me might flow.

Chapter 8

REST

Some years ago a gentleman came to me and asked me which I thought was the most precious promise of all those that Christ left. I took some time to look them over, but I gave it up. I found that I could not answer the question. It is like a man with a large family of children, he cannot tell which he likes best; he loves them all. But if not the best, this is one of the sweetest promises of all: "Come unto Me, all ye that labor and are heavy laden, and I will give you rest. Take my yoke upon you, and learn of Me, for I am meek and lowly in heart: and ye shall find rest unto your souls. For my yoke is easy, and My burden is light."

There are a good many people who think the promises are not going to be fulfilled. There are some that you do see fulfilled, and you cannot help but believe they are true. Now remember that all the promises are not given without conditions. Some are given with, and others without, conditions attached to them. For instance, it says, "If I regard iniquity in my heart, the Lord will not hear me." Now, I need not pray as long as I am cherishing some known sin. He will not hear me, much less answer me. The Lord says in the eighty fourth Psalm, "No good thing will he withhold from them that walk uprightly." If I am not walking uprightly I have no claims under the promise. Again, some of the promises were made to certain individuals or nations. For instance, God said that He would make Abraham's seed to multiply as the stars of heaven: but that is not a promise for you or me. Some promises were made to the Jews, and do not apply to the Gentiles.

Then there are promises without conditions. He promised Adam and Eve that the world should have a Savior, and there was no power in earth or perdition that could keep Christ from coming at the appointed time. When Christ left the world, He said He would send us the Holy Ghost. He had only been gone ten days when the Holy Ghost came. And so you can run right through the Scriptures, and you will find that some of the promises are with, and some without, conditions; and if we don't comply with the conditions we cannot expect them to be fulfilled.

I believe it will be the experience of every man and woman on the face of the earth, I believe that everyone will be obliged to testify in the evening of life, that if they have complied with the condition, the Lord has fulfilled His word to the letter. Joshua, the old Hebrew hero, was an illustration. After having tested God forty years in the Egyptian brick-kilns, forty years in the desert, and thirty years in the Promised Land, his dying testimony was: "Not one thing hath failed of all the good things which the Lord promised." I believe you could heave the ocean easier than break one of God's promises. So when we come to a promise like the one we have before us now, I want you to bear in mind that there is no discount upon it. "Come unto Me, all ye that labor and are heavy laden, and I will give you rest."

Perhaps you say: "I hope Mr. Moody is not going to preach on this old text." Yes: I am. When I take up an album, it does not interest me if all the photographs are new; but if I know any of the faces. I stop at once. So with these old, well-known texts. They have quenched our thirst before, but the water is still bubbling up — we cannot drink it dry.

If you probe the human heart, you will find a want, and that want is rest. The cry of the world to day is, "Where can rest be found?" Why are theaters and places of amusement crowded at night? What is the secret of Sunday driving, of the saloons and brothels? Some think they are going to get it in pleasure, others think they are going to get it in wealth, and others in literature. They are seeking and finding no rest.

Where Can Rest be Found?

If I wanted to find a person who had rest I would not go among the very wealthy. The man that we read of in the twelfth chapter of Luke, thought he was going to get rest by multiplying his goods, but he was disappointed. "Soul, take thine ease." I venture to say that there is not a person in this wide world who has tried to find rest in that way and found it.

Money cannot buy it. Many a millionaire would gladly give millions if he could purchase it as he does his stocks and shares. God has made the soul a little too large for this world. Roll the whole world in, and still there is room. There is care in getting wealth, and more care in keeping it.

Nor would I go among the pleasure seekers. They have a few hours' enjoyment, but the next day there is enough sorrow to counterbalance it. They may drink the cup of pleasure today, but the cup of pain comes on to-morrow.

To find rest I would never go among the politicians, or among the so-called great. Congress is the last place on earth that I would go. In the Lower House they want to go to the Senate; in the Senate they want to go to the Cabinet; and then they want to go to the White House; and rest has never been found there. Nor would I go among the halls of learning. "Much study is a weariness to the flesh." I would not go among the upper ten, the "bon-ton," for they are constantly chasing after fashion. Have you not noticed their troubled faces on our streets? And the face is index to the soul. They have no hopeful look. Their worship of pleasure is slavery. Solomon tried pleasure, and found bitter disappointment, and down the ages has come the bitter cry, "All is vanity."

Now, there is no rest in sin. The wicked know nothing about it. The Scriptures tell us the wicked "are like the troubled sea that cannot rest." You have, perhaps been on the sea when there is a calm, when the water is as clear as crystal, and it seemed as if the sea were at rest. But if you looked you would see that the waves came in, and that the calm was only on the surface. Man, like the sea, has no rest. He has had no rest since Adam fell, and there is none for him until he returns to God again, and the light of Christ shines into his heart.

Rest cannot be found in the world, and thank God the world cannot take it from the believing heart! Sin is the cause of all this unrest. It brought toil and labor and misery into the world.

Now for something positive. I would go successfully to someone who has heard the sweet voice of Jesus, and has laid his burden down at the cross. There is rest, sweet rest. Thousands could certify to this blessed fact. They could say, and truthfully:

> I heard the voice of Jesus say,
> "Come unto me and rest.
> Lay down, thou weary one, lay down,
> Thy head upon my breast."
> I came to Jesus as I was,
> Weary and worn and sad.
> I found in Him a resting-place,
> And He hath made me glad.

Among all his writings St. Augustine has nothing sweeter than this: "Thou hast made us for Thyself, O God, and our heart is restless till it rests in Thee."

Do you know that for four thousand years no prophet or priest or patriarch ever stood up and uttered a text like this? It would be blasphemy for Moses to have uttered a text like it. Do you think he had rest when he was teasing the Lord to let him go into the Promised Land? Do you think Elijah could have uttered such a text as this, when, under the juniper-tree, he prayed that he might die? And this is one of the strongest proofs that Jesus Christ was not only man, but God. He was God-Man, and this is Heaven's proclamation, "Come unto Me, and I will give you rest". He brought it down from heaven with Him.

Now, if this text was not true, don't you think it would have been found out by this time? I believe it as much as I believe in my existence. Why? Because I not only find it in the Book, but in my own experience. The "I wills" of Christ have never been broken, and never can be.

I thank God for the word "give" in that passage. He doesn't sell it. Some of us are so poor that we could not buy it if it was for sale. Thank God, we can get it for nothing.

I like to have a text like this, because it takes us all in. "Come unto me all ye that labor." That doesn't mean a select few — refined ladies and cultured men. It doesn't mean good people only. It applies to saint and sinner. Hospitals are for the sick, not for healthy people. Do you think that Christ would shut the door in anyone's face, and say, "I did not mean all; I only meant certain ones"? If you cannot come as a saint, come as a sinner. Only come!

A lady told me once that she was so hard-hearted she couldn't come.

"Well," I said, "my good woman, it doesn't say all ye soft-hearted people come. Black hearts, vile hearts, hard hearts, soft hearts, all hearts come. Who can soften your hard heart but Himself?"

The harder the heart, the more need you have to come. If my watch stops I don't take it to a drug store or to a blacksmith's shop, but to the watchmaker's, to have it repaired. So if the heart gets out of order take it to its keeper, Christ, to have it set right. If you can prove that you are a sinner, you are entitled to the promise. Get all the benefit you can out of it.

Now, there are a good many believers who think this text applies only to sinners; It is just the thing for them too. What do we see today? The Church, Christian people, all loaded down with cares and troubles. "Come unto me all ye that labor." All! I believe that includes the Christian whose heart is burdened with some great sorrow. The Lord wants you to come.

Christ the Burden-Bearer

It says in another place, "Casting all your care upon Him, for He careth for you." We would have a victorious Church if we could get Christian people to realize that. But they have never made the discovery. They agree that Christ is the sin-bearer, but they do not realize that He is also the burden-bearer. "Surely He hath borne our griefs and carried our sorrows." It is the privilege of every child of God to walk in unclouded sunlight.

Some people go back into the past and rake up all the troubles they ever had, and then they look into the future and anticipate that they will have still more trouble, and they go reeling and staggering all through life. They give you the cold chills every time they meet you. They put on a whining voice, and tell you what "a hard time they have had." I believe they embalm them, and bring out the mummy on every opportunity. The Lord says, "Cast all your care on Me. I want to carry your burdens and your troubles." What we want is a joyful Church, and we are not going to convert the world until we have it. We want to get this long-faced Christianity off the face of the earth.

Take these people that have some great burden, and let them come into a meeting. If you can get their attention upon the singing or preaching, they will say, "Oh, wasn't it grand! I forgot all my cares." And they just drop their bundle at the end of the pew. But the moment the benediction is pronounced they grab the bundle again. You laugh, but you do it yourself. Cast your care on Him.

Sometimes they go into their closet and close their door, and they get so carried away and lifted up that they forget their trouble; but they just take it up again the moment they get off their knees. Leave your sorrow now; cast all your care upon Him. If you cannot come to Christ as a saint, come as a sinner. But if you are a saint with some trouble or care, bring it to Him. Saint and sinner, come! He wants you all. Don't let Satan deceive you into believing that you cannot come if you will. Christ says, "Ye will not come unto Me." With the command comes the power.

A man in one of our meetings in Europe said he would like to come, but he was chained, and couldn't come.

A Scotchman said to him, "Ay, man, why don't you come chain and all?"

He said, "I never thought of that."

Are you cross and peevish, and do you make things unpleasant at home? My friend, come to Christ and ask Him to help you. Whatever the sin is, bring it to Him.

What Does it Mean to Come?

Perhaps you say, "Mr. Moody, I wish you would tell us what it is to come." I have given up trying to explain it. I always feel like the colored minister who said he was going to confound, instead of expound, the chapter.

The best definition is just — come. The more you try to explain it, the more you are mystified. About the first thing a mother teaches her child is to look. She takes the baby to the window, and says, "Look, baby, papa is coming!" Then she teaches the child to come. She props it up against a chair, and says, "Come!" and by and by the little thing pushes the chair along towards mamma. That's coming. You don't need to go to college to learn how. You don't need any minister to tell you what it is. Now will you come to Christ? He said, "Him that cometh unto Me, I will in no wise cast out."

When we have such a promise as this, let us cling to it, and never give it up. Christ is not mocking us. He wants us to come with all our sins and backslidings, and throw ourselves upon His bosom. It is our sins God wants, not our tears only. They alone do no good. And we cannot come through resolutions. Action is necessary. How many times at church have we said, "I will turn over a new leaf," but the Monday leaf is worse than the Saturday leaf.

The way to heaven is straight as a rule, but it is the way of the cross. Don't try to get around it. Shall I tell you what the "yoke" referred to in the text is? It is the cross which Christians must bear. The only way by which you can find rest in this dark world is by taking up the yoke of Christ. I do not know what it may include in your case, beyond taking up your Christian duties, acknowledging Christ and acting as becomes one of His disciples. Perhaps it may be to erect a gamily altar; or to tell a godless husband that you have made up your mind to serve God; or to tell your parents that you want to be a Christian. Follow the will of God, and happiness and peace and rest will come. The way of obedience is always the way of blessing.

I was preaching in Chicago to a hall full of women one Sunday afternoon, and after the meeting was over a lady came to me and said she wanted to talk to me. She said she would accept Christ, and after some conversation she went home. I looked for her for a whole week, but didn't see her until the following Sunday afternoon. She came and sat down right in front of me, and her face had such a sad expression. She seemed to have entered into the misery, instead of the joy, of the Lord.

After the meeting was over I went to her and asked her what the trouble was.

She said: "Oh, Mr. Moody, this has been the most miserable week of my life."

I asked her if there was anyone with whom she had had trouble and whom she could not forgive.

She said: "No, not that I know of."

"Well, did you tell your friends about having found the Savior?"

"Indeed I didn't, I have been all the week trying to keep it from them."

"Well," I said, "that is the reason why you have no peace."

She wanted to take the crown, but did not want the cross. My friends, you must go by the way of Calvary. If you ever get rest, you must get it at the foot of the cross.

"Why," she said, "if I should go home and tell my infidel husband that I had found Christ I don't know what he would do. I think he would turn me out."

"Well," I said, "go out."

She went away, promising that she would tell him, timid and pale, but she did not want another wretched week. She was bound to have peace.

The next night I gave a lecture to men only, and in the hall there were eight thousand men and one solitary woman. When I got through and went into the inquiry meeting, I found this lady with her husband. She introduced him to me (he was a doctor, and a very influential man) and said:

"He wants to become a Christian."

I took my Bible and told him all about Christ, and he accepted Him. I said to her after it was all over:

"It turned out quite differently from what you expected, didn't it?"

"Yes," she replied, "I was never so scared in my life. I expected he would do something dreadful, but it has turned out so well."

She took God's way, and got rest.

I want to say to young ladies, perhaps you have a godless father or mother, a sceptical brother, who is going down through drink, and perhaps there is no one who can reach them but you. How many times a godly, pure young lady has taken the light into some darkened home! Many a home might be lit up with the Gospel if the mothers and daughters would only speak the word.

The last time Mr. Sankey and myself were in Edinburgh, there were a father, two sisters and a brother, who used every morning to take the morning paper and pick my sermon to pieces. They were indignant to think that the Edinburgh people should be carried away with such preaching. One day one of the sisters was going by the hall, and she thought she would drop in and see what class of people went there. She happened to take a seat by a godly lady, who said to her:

"I hope you are interested in this work."

She tossed her head and said: "Indeed I am not. I am disgusted with everything I have seen and heard."

"Well," said the lady, "perhaps you came prejudiced."

"Yes, and the meeting has not removed any of it, but has rather increased it."

"I have received a great deal of good from them."

"There is nothing here for me. I don't see how an intellectual person can be interested."

To make a long story short, she got the lady to promise to come back. When the meeting broke up, just a little of the prejudice had worn away. She promised to come back again the next day, and then she attended three or four more meetings, and became quite interested. She said nothing to her family, until finally the burden became too heavy, and she told them. They laughed at her, and made her the butt of their ridicule.

One day the two sisters were together, and the other said: "Now what have you got at those meetings that you didn't have in the first place?"

"I have a peace that I never knew of before. I am at peace with God, myself and all the world." Did you ever have a little war of your own with your neighbors, in your own family? And she said: "I have self-control. You know, sister, if you had said half the mean things before I was converted that you have said since, I would have been angry and answered back, but if you remember correctly, I haven't answered once since I have been converted."

The sister said: "You certainly have something that I have not." The other told her it was for her too, and she brought the sister to the meetings, where she found peace.

Like Martha and Mary, they had a brother, but he was a member of the University of Edinburgh. He be converted? He go to these meetings? It might do for women, but not for him. One night they came home and told him that a chum of his own, a member of the University, had stood up and confessed Christ, and when he sat down his brother got up and confessed; and so with the third one.

When the young man heard it, he said: "Do you mean to tell me that he has been converted?"

"Yes."

"Well," he said, "there must be something in it."

He put on his hat, and coat, and went to see his friend Black. Black got him down to the meetings, and he was converted.

We went through to Glasgow, and had not been there six weeks when news came that that young man had been stricken down and died. When he was dying he called his father to his bedside and said:

"Wasn't it a good thing that my sisters went to those meetings? Won't you meet me in heaven, father?"

"Yes, my son, I am so glad you are a Christian; that is the only comfort that I have in losing you. I will become a Christian, and will meet you again."

I tell this to encourage some sister to go home and carry the message of salvation. It may be that your brother may be taken away in a few months. My dear friends, are we not living in solemn days? Isn't it time for us to get our friends into the Kingdom of God? Come, wife, won't you tell your husband? Come, sister, won't you tell your brother? Won't you take up your cross now? The blessing of God will rest on your soul if you will.

I was in Wales once, and a lady told me this little story: An English friend of hers, a mother, had a child that was sick. At first they considered there was no danger, until one day the doctor came in and said that the symptoms were very unfavorable. He took the mother out of the room, and told her that the child could not live. It came like a thunderbolt. After the doctor had gone the mother went into the room where the child lay and began to talk to the child and tried to divert its mind.

"Darling, do you know you will soon hear the music of heaven? You will hear a sweeter song than you have ever heard on earth. You will hear them sing the song of Moses and the Lamb. You are very fond of music. Won't it be sweet, darling?"

And the little tired, sick child turned its head away, and said, "Oh mamma, I am so tired and so sick that I think it would make me worse to hear all that music."

"Well," the mother said, "you will soon see Jesus, You will see the seraphim and cherubim and the streets all paved with gold"; and she went on picturing heaven as it is described in Revelation.

The little tired child again turned its head away, and said, "Oh mamma, I am so tired that I think it would make me worse to see all those beautiful things!"

At last the mother took the child up in her arms, and pressed her to her loving heart. And the little sick one whispered:

"Oh mamma, that is what I want. If Jesus will only take me in His arms and let me rest!"

Dear friend, are you not tired and weary of sin? Are you not weary of the turmoil of life? You can end rest on the bosom of the Son of God.

Chapter 9

SEVEN "I WILLS" OF CHRIST

A man when he says "I will," may not mean much. We very often say "I will," when we don't mean to fulfil what we say; but when we come to the "I will" of Christ, He means to fulfil it. Everything He has promised to do, He is able and willing to accomplish; and He is going to do it. I cannot find any passage in Scripture in which He says "I will" do this, or "I will" do that, but it will be done.

1. The "I Will" of Salvation

The first "I will" to which I want to direct your attention, is to be found in John's gospel, sixth chapter and thirty-seventh verse: "Him that cometh unto Me I will in no wise cast out."

I imagine someone will say, "Well, if I was what I ought to be, I would come; but when my mind goes over the past record of my life, it is too dark. I am not fit to come."

You must bear in mind that Jesus Christ came to save not good people, not the upright and just, but sinners like you and me, who have gone astray, and sinned and come short of the glory of God. Listen to this "I will" — it goes right into the heart — "Him that cometh unto Me, I will in no wise cast out." Surely that is broad enough — is it not? I don't care who the man or woman is; I don't care what their trials, what their troubles, what their sorrows, or what their sins are, if they will only come straight to the Master, He will not cast them out. Come then, poor sinner; come just as you are, and take Him at His word.

He is so anxious to save sinners, He will take everyone who comes. He will take those who are so full of sin that they are despised by all who know them, who have been rejected by their fathers and mothers, who have been cast off by the wives of their bosoms. He will take those who have sunk so low that upon them no eye of pity is cast. His occupation is to hear and save. That is what He left heaven and came into the world for; that is what He left the throne of God for — to save sinners. "The Son of man is come to seek and to save that which was lost." He did not come to condemn the world but that the world through Him might be saved.

A wild and prodigal young man, who was running a headlong career to ruin came into one of our meetings in Chicago. The Spirit of God got hold of him. Whilst I was conversing with him, and endeavoring to bring him to Christ, I quoted this verse to him.

I asked him: "Do you believe Christ said that?"

"I suppose He did."

"Suppose He did! do you believe it?"

"I hope so."

"Hope so! do you believe it? You do your work, and the Lord will do His. Just come as you are, and throw yourself upon His bosom, and He will not cast you out."

This man thought it was too simple and easy.

At last light seemed to break in upon him, and he seemed to find comfort from it. It was past midnight before he got down on his knees, but down he went, and was converted. I said:

"Now, don't think you are going to get out of the devil's territory without trouble. The devil will come to you to-morrow morning, and say it was all feeling; that you only imagined you were accepted by God. When he does, don't fight him with your own opinions, but fight him with John 6:37: 'Him that cometh to Me I will in no wise cast out.' Let that be the 'sword of the Spirit.'"

I don't believe that any man ever starts to go to Christ, but the devil strives somehow or other to meet him and trip him up. And even after he has come to Christ, the devil tries to assail him with doubts, and make him believe there is something wrong in it.

The struggle came sooner than I thought in this man's case. When he was on his way home the devil assailed him. He used this text, but the devil put this thought into his mind: "How do you know Christ ever said that after all? Perhaps the translators made a mistake."

Into darkness he went again. He was in trouble till about two in the morning. At last he came to this conclusion. Said he:

"I will believe it anyway; and when I get to heaven, if it isn't true, I will just tell the Lord I didn't make the mistake — the translators made it."

The kings and princes of this world, when they issue invitations, call round them the rich, the mighty and powerful, the honorable and the wise; but the Lord, when He was on earth; called round Him the vilest of the vile. That was the principal fault the people found with Him. Those self-righteous Pharisees were not going to associate with harlots and publicans. The principal charge against Him was: "This man receiveth sinners and eateth with them." Who would have such a man around him as John Bunyan in his time? He, a Bedford tinker, couldn't get inside one of the princely castles. I was very much amused when I was over on the other side. They had erected a monument to John Bunyan, and it was unveiled by lords and dukes and great men. While he was on earth, they would not have allowed him inside the walls of their castles. Yet he was made one of the mightiest instruments in the spread of the Gospel. No book that has ever been written comes so near the Bible as John Bunyan's "Pilgrim's Progress." And he was a poor Bedford tinker. So it is with God. He picks up some poor, lost tramp, and makes him an instrument to turn hundreds and thousands to Christ.

George Whitefield, standing in his tabernacle in London, and with a multitude gathered about him, cried out: "The Lord Jesus will save the devil's castaways!"

Two poor abandoned wretches standing outside in the street, heard him, as his silvery voice rang out on the air. Looking into each other's faces, they said: "That must mean you and me." They wept and rejoiced. They drew near and looked in at the door, at the face of the earnest messenger, the tears streaming from his eyes as he plead with the people to give their hearts to God. One of them wrote him a little note and sent it to him.

Later that day, as he sat at the table of Lady Huntington, who was his special friend, someone present said:

"Mr. Whitefield, did you not go a little too far today when you said that the Lord would save the devil's castaways?"

Taking the note from his pocket he gave it to the lady, and said: "Will you read that note aloud?"

She read: "Mr. Whitefield: Two poor lost women stood outside your tabernacle today, and heard you say that the Lord would save the devil's castaways. We seized upon that as our last hope, and we write you this to tell you that we rejoice now in believing in Him, and from this good hour we shall endeavor to serve Him, who has done so much for us."

2. The "I Will" of Cleansing

The next "I will" is found in Luke, fifth chapter. We read of a leper who came to Christ, and said: "Lord, if Thou wilt, Thou canst make me clean." The Lord touched him, saying, "I will: be thou clean"; and immediately the leprosy left him.

Now if any man or woman full of the leprosy of sin read this, if you will but go to the Master and tell all your case to Him, He will speak to you as He did to that poor leper and say. "I will: be thou clean," and the leprosy of your sins will flee away from you. It is the Lord, and the Lord alone, who can forgive sins. If you say to Him, "Lord, I am full of sin; Thou canst make me clean"; "Lord, I have a terrible temper; Thou canst make me clean"; "Lord, I have a deceitful heart. Cleanse me, O Lord; give me a new heart. O Lord, give me the power to overcome the flesh, and the snares of the devil!"; "Lord, I am full of unclean habits"; if you come to Him with a sincere spirit, you will hear the voice, "I will; be thou clean." It will be done. Do you think that the God who created the world out of nothing, who by a breath put life into the world — do you think that if He says, "Thou shalt be clean," you will not?

Now, you can make a wonderful exchange today. You can have health in the place of sickness; you can get rid of everything that is vile and hateful in the sight of God. The Son of God comes down, and says, "I will take away your leprosy, and give you health in its stead. I will take away that terrible disease that is ruining your body and soul, and give you my righteousness in its stead. I will clothe you with the garments of salvation."

Is it not wonderful? That's what He means when He says — I will. Oh, lay hold of this "I will!"

3. The "I Will" of Confession

Now turn to Matthew, tenth chapter, thirty-second verse: "Whosoever therefore shall confess Me before men, him will I confess also before my Father which is in heaven." There's the "I will" of confession.

Now, that's the next thing that takes place after a man is saved. When we have been washed in the blood of the Lamb, the next thing is to get our mouths opened. We have to confess Christ here in this dark world, and tell His love to others. We are not to be ashamed of the Son of God.

A man thinks it a great honor when he has achieved a victory that causes his name to be mentioned in the English Parliament, or in the presence of the Queen and her court. How excited we used to be during the war, when some general did something extraordinary, and someone got up in Congress to confess his exploits; how the papers used to talk about it! In China, we read, the highest ambition of the successful soldier is to have his name written in the palace or temple of Confucius. But just think of having your name mentioned in the kingdom of heaven by the Prince of Glory, by the Son of God, because you confess Him here on earth! You confess Him here; He will confess you yonder.

If you wish to be brought into the clear light of liberty, you must take your stand on Christ's side. I have known many Christians go groping about in darkness, and never get into the clear light of the kingdom, because they were ashamed to confess the Son of God. We are living in a day when men want a religion without the cross. They want the crown, but not the cross. But if we are to be disciples of Jesus Christ, we have to take up our crosses daily — not once a year, or on the Sabbath, but daily. And if we take up our crosses and follow Him, we shall be blessed in the very act.

I remember a man in New York who used to come and pray with me. He had his cross. He was afraid to confess Christ. It seemed that down at the bottom of his trunk he had a Bible. He wanted to get it out and read it to the companion with whom he lived, but he was ashamed to do it. For a whole week that was his cross; and after he had carried the burden that long, and after a terrible struggle, he made up his mind. He said, "I will take my Bible out tonight and read it." He took it out, and soon he heard the footsteps of his mate coming upstairs.

His first impulse was to put it away again, but then he thought he would not — he would face his companion with it. His mate came in, and seeing him at his Bible, said,

"John, are you interested in these things?" "Yes," he replied.

"How long has this been, then?" asked his companion.

"Exactly a week," he answered; "for a whole week I have tried to get out my Bible to read to you, but I have never done so till now."

"Well," said his friend, "it is a strange thing. I was converted on the some night, and I too was ashamed to take my Bible out."

You are ashamed to take your Bible out and say, "I have lived a godless life for all these years, but I will commence now to live a life of righteousness." You are ashamed to open your Bible and read that blessed Psalm, "The Lord is my Shepherd, I shall not want." You are ashamed to be seen on your knees. No man can be a disciple of Jesus Christ without bearing His cross. A great many people want to know how it is Jesus Christ has so few disciples, whilst Mahomet has so many. The reason is that Mahomet gives no cross to bear. There are so few men who will come out to take their stand.

I was struck during the American war with the fact that there were so many men who could go to the cannon's mouth without trembling, but who had not courage to take up their Bibles to read them at night. They were ashamed of the Gospel of Jesus Christ, which is the power of God unto salvation. "Whosoever therefore shall confess me before men, him will I confess also before My Father which is in heaven. But whosoever shall deny Me before men, him will I also deny before My Father which is in heaven."

4. The "I Will" of Service

The next I will is the "I will" of service.

There are a good many Christians who have been quickened and aroused to say, "I want to do some service for Christ."

Well, Christ says, "Follow Me, and I will make you fishers of men."

There is no Christian who cannot help to bring someone to the Savior. Christ says, "And I, if I be lifted up, will draw all men unto Me"; and our business is just to lift up Christ.

Our Lord said, "Follow Me, Peter, and I will make you a fisher of men"; and Peter simply obeyed Him, and there, on that day of Pentecost, we see the result. Peter had a good haul on the day of Pentecost. I doubt if he ever caught so many fish in one day as he did men on that day. It would have broken every net they had on board, if they had had to drag up three thousand fishes.

I read some time ago of a man who took passage in a stage coach. There were first, second and third-class passengers. But when he looked into the coach, he saw all the passengers sitting together without distinction. He could not understand it till by-and-by they came to a hill, and the coach stopped, and the driver called out, "First-class passengers keep their seats, second-class passengers get out and walk, third class passengers get behind and push." Now in the Church we have no room for first-class passengers — people who think that salvation means an easy ride all the way to heaven. We have no room for second class passengers — people who are carried most of the time, and who, when they must work out their own salvation, go trudging on giving never a thought to helping their fellows along.

All church members ought to be third class passengers — ready to dismount and push all together, and push with a will. That was John Wesley's definition of a church — "All at it, and always at it." Every Christian ought to be a worker. He need not be a preacher, he need not be an evangelist, to be useful. He may be useful in business. See what power an employer has, if he likes! How he could labor with his employees, and in his business relations! Often a man can be far more useful in a business sphere than he could in another.

There is one reason, and a great reason, why so many do not succeed. I have been asked by a great many good men, "Why is it we don't have any results? We work hard, pray hard, and preach hard, and yet the success does not come." I will tell you. It is because they spend all their time mending their nets. No wonder they never catch anything.

The great matter is to hold inquiry meetings, and thus pull the net in, and see if you have caught anything. If you are always mending and setting the net, you won't catch many fish. Whoever heard of a man going out to fish, and setting his net, and then letting it stop there, and never pulling it in? Everybody would laugh at the man's folly.

A minister in England came to me one day, and said, "I wish you would tell me why we ministers don't succeed better than we do."

I brought before him this idea of pulling in the net, and I said, "You ought to pull in your nets. There are many ministers in Manchester who can preach much better than I can, but I pull in the net."

Many people have objections to inquiry meetings, but I urged upon him the importance of them, and the minister said,

"I never did pull in my net, but I will try next Sunday."

He did so, and eight persons, anxious inquirers, went into his study. The next Sunday he came down to see me, and said he had never had such a Sunday in his life. He had met with marvelous blessing. The next time he drew the net there were forty, and when he came to see me later, he said to me joyfully,

"Moody, I have had eight hundred conversions this last year! It is a great mistake I did not begin earlier to pull in the net."

So, my friends, if you want to catch men, just pull in the net. If you only catch one, it will be something. It may be a little child, but I have known a little child to convert a whole family. You don't know what is in that little dull-headed boy in the inquiry-room; he may become a Martin Luther, a reformer that shall make the world tremble — you cannot tell. God uses the weak things of this world to confound the mighty. God's promise is as good as a bank note — "I promise to pay So-and-So," and here is one of Christ's promissory notes — "If you follow Me, I will make you fishers of men." Will you not lay hold of the promise, and trust it, and follow Him now?

If a man preaches the Gospel, and preaches it faithfully, he ought to expect results then and there. I believe it is the privilege of God's children to reap the fruit of their labor three hundred and sixty five days in the year.

"Well, but," say some, "is there not a sowing time as well as harvest?"

Yes, it is true, there is; but then, you can sow with one hand, and reap with the other. What would you think of a farmer who went on sowing all the year round, and never thought of reaping? I repeat it, we want to sow with one hand, and reap with the other; and if we look for the fruit of our labors, we shall see it. "I, if I be lifted up, will draw all men unto Me." We must lift Christ up, and then seek men out, and bring them to Him.

You must use the right kind of bait. A good many don't do this, and then they wonder they are not successful. You see them getting up all kinds of entertainments with which to try and catch men. They go the wrong way to work. This perishing world wants Christ, and Him crucified. There's a void in every man's bosom that wants filling up, and if we only approach him with the right kind of bait, we shall catch him. This poor world needs a Savior; and if we are going to be successful in catching men, we must preach Christ crucified — not His life only but His death. And if we are only faithful in doing this, we shall succeed. And why? Because there is His promise: "If you follow Me, I will make you fishers of men." That promise holds just as good to you and me as it did to His disciples, and is as true now as it was in their time.

Think of Paul up yonder. People are going up every day and every hour, men and women who have been brought to Christ through his writings. He set streams in motion that have flowed on for more than a thousand years. I can imagine men going up there, and saying, "Paul, I thank you for writing that letter to the Ephesians; I found Christ in that." "Paul, I thank you for writing that epistle to the Corinthians." "Paul, I found Christ in that epistle to the Philippians." "I thank you, Paul, for that epistle to the Galatians; I found Christ in that." And so, I suppose, they are going up still, thanking Paul all the while for what he had done. Ah, when Paul was put in prison he did not fold his hands and sit down in idleness! No, he began to write; and his epistles have come down through the long ages of time, and brought thousands on thousands to a knowledge of Christ crucified. Yes, Christ said to Paul, "I will make you a fisher of men if you will follow Me," and he has been fishing for souls ever since. The devil thought he had done a very wise thing when he got Paul into prison, but he was very much mistaken; he overdid it for once. I have no doubt Paul has thanked God ever since for that Philippian gaol, and his stripes and imprisonment there. I am sure the world has made more by it than we shall ever know till we get to heaven.

5. The "I Will" of Comfort

The next "I will" is in John, fourteenth chapter, verse eighteen: "I will not leave you comfortless."

To me it is a sweet thought that Christ has not left us alone in this dark wilderness here below. Although He has gone up on high, and taken His seat by the Father's throne, He has not left us comfortless. The better translation is, "I will not leave you orphans." He did not leave Joseph when they cast him into prison. "God was with him." When Daniel was cast into the den of lions, they had to put the Almighty in with him. They were so bound together that they could not be separated, and so God went down into the den of lions with Daniel.

If we have got Christ with us, we can do all things. Do not let us be thinking how weak we are. Let us lift up our eyes to Him, and think of Him as our Elder Brother, who has all power given to Him in heaven and on earth. He says: "Lo, I am with you alway, even unto the end of the world." Some of our children and friends leave us, and it is a very sad hour. But, thank God, the believer and Christ shall never be separated! He is with us here, and we shall be with Him in person by and by, and shall see Him in His beauty. But not only is He with us, but He has sent us the Holy Ghost. Let us honor the Holy Ghost by acknowledging that He is here in our midst. He has power to give sight to the blind, liberty to the captive, and to open the ears of the deaf that they may hear the glorious words of the Gospel.

6. The "I Will" of Resurrection

Then there is another I will in John, sixth chapter, verse forty; it occurs four times in the chapter: "I will raise him up at the last day."

I rejoice to think that I have a Savior who has power over death. My blessed Master holds the keys him, and I got more comfort out of that promise "I will raise him up at the last day," than anything else in the Bible. How it cheered me! How it lighted up my path! And as I went into the room and looked upon the lovely face of that brother, how that passage ran through my soul: "Thy brother shall rise again." I said, "Thank God for that promise." It was worth more than the world to me.

When we laid him in the grave, it seemed as if I could hear the voice of Jesus Christ saying, "Thy brother shall rise again." Blessed promise of the resurrection! Blessed "I will!" "I will raise him up at the last day."

7. The "I Will" of Glory

Now the next I will is in John, seventeenth chapter, twenty-fourth verse: "Father, I will that they also, whom Thou hast given Me, be with Me where I am."

This was in His last prayer in the guest-chamber, on the last night before He was crucified and died that terrible death on Calvary. Many a believer's countenance begins to light up at the thought that he shall see the King in His beauty by and by. Yes; there is a glorious day before us in the future. Some think that on the first day we are converted we have got everything. To be sure, we get salvation for the past and peace for the present; but then there is the glory for the future in store. That's what kept Paul rejoicing. He said, "These light afflictions, these few stripes, these few brickbats and stones that they throw at me — why, the glory that is beyond excels them so much that I count them as nothing, nothing at all, so that I may win Christ." And so, when things go against us, let us cheer up; let us remember that the night will soon pass away, and the morning dawn upon us. Death never comes there. It is banished from that heavenly land. Sickness, and pain, and sorrow, come not there to mar that grand and glorious home where we shall be by and by with the Master. God's family will be all together there. Glorious future, my friends! Yes, glorious day! and it may be a great deal nearer than many of us think. During these few days we are here let us stand steadfast and firm, and by and by we shall be in the unbroken circle in yon world of light, and have the King in our midst.

www.ingramcontent.com/pod-product-compliance
Lightning Source LLC
Chambersburg PA
CBHW070602010526
44118CB00012B/1424